Mapping and Visualization with SuperCollider

Create interactive and responsive audio-visual
applications with SuperCollider

Marinos Koutsomichalis

BIRMINGHAM - MUMBAI

Mapping and Visualization with SuperCollider

First published: November 2013

Production Reference: 1191113

Published by Packt Publishing Ltd.
Livery Place
35 Livery Street
Birmingham B3 2PB, UK.

ISBN 978-1-78328-967-7

www.packtpub.com

Cover Image by Aniket Sawant (aniket_sawant_photography@hotmail.com)

Credits

Author
Marinos Koutsomichalis

Reviewers
João Martinho Moura
Joshua Parmenter
Phil Thomson

Acquisition Editor
Vinay Argekar

Commissioning Editor
Poonam Jain

Technical Editors
Kunal Anil Gaikwad
Iram Malik
Shruti Rawool

Copy Editors
Roshni Banerjee
Gladson Monteiro
Deepa Nambiar
Karuna Narayanan
Shambhavi Pai

Project Coordinator
Joel Goveya

Proofreaders
Mario Cecere
Stephen Copestake

Indexer
Monica Ajmera Mehta

Graphics
Ronak Dhruv
Abhinash Sahu

Production Coordinator
Pooja Chiplunkar

Cover Work
Pooja Chiplunkar

About the Author

Marinos Koutsomichalis (Athens, 1981) is an artist and scholar working with sound and a wide range of other media. His artistic work interrogates the specifics of site, perception, technology, and material. His academic interests include computer programming, generative art, new aesthetics, and environmental sound and noise. He has widely performed, exhibited, and lectured internationally and has held residencies in miscellaneous research centers and institutions. He has an MA by research in composition with digital media by the University of York and, as of writing, he is a candidate PhD in Music, Sound, and Media Art at the De Montfort University. He is in the board of the Contemporary Music Research Center (KSYME-CMRC) and also the director of its class of Electronic Music and Sound Synthesis. As of writing, he is a research fellow in the University of Turin.

I would like to thank Packt Publishing for offering me the amazing opportunity to write this book, and in particular Shreerang Deshpande, Joel Goveya, Poonam Jain, Kunal Anil Gaikwad, Iram Malik, and Shruti Rawool for guiding me through the complexities of such a task. I would also like to thank the reviewers of this title, namely Josh Parmenter, João Martinho Moura, and Phil Thomson, for their invaluable comments and suggestions. I would also like to thank my parents, Anna and Georgios, as well as my sister, Danai, for their long term understanding and support. Part of this book was written in Milatos, North Crete, while being accommodated by my partner's parents, Maria and Michalis, who deserve a special mention for making me feel comfortable during my stay there. Last but not least, I would like to express my profound gratitude towards my partner, Phaedra Logariastaki, for her unconditional support and for spending the whole of her summer vacations watching me sitting in front of a laptop instead of being with her. Without the support of all these people, this book would have been impossible to finish.

About the Reviewers

João Martinho Moura is a researcher and media artist born in Portugal. His interests lie in digital art, intelligent interfaces, digital music, and computational aesthetics. He was invited as a professor at the Master Program in Technology and Digital Arts at the University of Minho, Portugal, teaching Programming for Digital Arts.

In 2013, he received the *National Multimedia Award-Art & Culture* from the APMP Multimedia Association in Portugal.

He has presented his work and research in a variety of conferences related to arts and technology, including:

- The International Festival for the Post-Digital Creation Culture OFFF (2008)
- World Congress on Communication and Arts (2010)
- SHiFT—Social and Human Ideas for Technology (2009)
- International Symposium on Computational Aesthetics in Graphics, Visualization, and Imaging CAe (2008)
- ARTECH (2008)
- ARTECH (2010)
- Computer Interaction (2009)
- ZON Digital Games (2007)
- International Creative Arts Fair (2008)
- ZON Multimédia Premium (2008)
- Le Corps Numérique-entre Culturel Saint-Exupéry (2011)
- Semibreve Award (2012)
- TEI International Conference on Tangible, Embedded, and Embodied Interaction (2011)
- Guimarães European Capital of Culture 2012

- Bodycontrolled Series LEAP — Lab for Electronic Arts and Performance Berlin (2012)
- Future Places (2012)
- The Ars Electronica Animation Festival (2012)
- SLSA Conference-Society for Literature, Science, and the Arts (2013), xCoAx — Computation Communication Aesthetics and X (2013)

His work has been presented in a variety of places in Portugal, Italy, USA, Brazil, UK, France, Hong Kong, Belgium, Germany, Israel, Spain, and Austria.

He is a researcher at engageLab, a laboratory at the intersection of arts and technology, established by two research centers at University of Minho, the Centre for Communication and Society Studies and the Centre Algoritmi.

I would like to thank the engageLab laboratory, at University of Minho, with a special mention to Pedro Branco and Nelson Zagalo.

Joshua Parmenter is a composer and performer of contemporary music with a focus on interactive live electronics. His works have been performed throughout America and Europe. Over the past decade, he has also been one of the developers in the open-source SuperCollider project. He also contributed to the *SuperCollider Book* available from MIT Press.

Phil Thomson is a Vancouver-based listener, composer, and writer/editor. His works have been heard in concerts and broadcasts in Canada, US, and abroad. His works for dance routines have been integrated with performances by choreographers, such as Jennifer Clarke Arora, James Gnam, and Sara Coffin. His writings have been published online by the Canadian Electroacoustic Community and in print by the Cambridge University Press.

www.PacktPub.com

Support files, eBooks, discount offers and more

You might want to visit www.PacktPub.com for support files and downloads related to your book.

Did you know that Packt offers eBook versions of every book published, with PDF and ePub files available? You can upgrade to the eBook version at www.PacktPub. com and as a print book customer, you are entitled to a discount on the eBook copy. Get in touch with us at service@packtpub.com for more details.

At www.PacktPub.com, you can also read a collection of free technical articles, sign up for a range of free newsletters and receive exclusive discounts and offers on Packt books and eBooks.

http://PacktLib.PacktPub.com

Do you need instant solutions to your IT questions? PacktLib is Packt's online digital book library. Here, you can access, read and search across Packt's entire library of books.

Why Subscribe?

- Fully searchable across every book published by Packt
- Copy and paste, print and bookmark content
- On demand and accessible via web browser

Free Access for Packt account holders

If you have an account with Packt at www.PacktPub.com, you can use this to access PacktLib today and view nine entirely free books. Simply use your login credentials for immediate access.

Table of Contents

Preface

Welcome to the *Mapping and Visualization with SuperCollider* book. As of this writing, SuperCollider is almost two decades old and has already proven itself as a solid, state-of-the-art environment for all sorts of audio-oriented applications. Albeit, SuperCollider is primarily known as a sound synthesis environment; it does feature a powerful graphics engine and, to a certain extent, is an excellent choice for prototyping and implementing visual and audiovisual applications. This may come as a surprise to some, given that there does exist an abundance of specialized environments and frameworks out there; many of them are also more featured and optimized than SuperCollider will ever be. Nonetheless, and at least as far as visualization is concerned, the latter constitutes a very rational choice, as it exhibits several advantages over the former. Namely, it features one of the most powerful sound synthesis engines available on the planet; it has a powerful interpreted, dynamic, object-oriented, and quite easy-to-learn high-level programming language; it has built-in features to facilitate algorithmic music composition, which can easily integrate with computer graphics; it is easy to learn and use compared to other specialized frameworks; and it is relatively fast and stable.

This book pinpoints mapping and visualization with SuperCollider. It elaborates both fundamental and more advanced techniques and illustrates how SuperCollider can offer solutions to a wide range of typical mapping/visualization scenarios, varying from very rudimentary to highly complex ones. The explicit focus herein is mapping and visualization, yet a wide range of prerequisites, or merely relevant to the latter topics are discussed; these include sonification, generative art, statistical analysis, communication protocols, automata, and neural networks. These are all approached practically and from a hands-on perspective through numerous examples. Notwithstanding, theoretical issues are also discussed whenever appropriate, so that the reader develops a more in-depth understanding of the various topics. Throughout this book, the importance of object modeling is explicitly highlighted too, and software architecture itself is elaborated upon. In general, these are very important aspects of programming and given the minimal, or even nonexistent, presence of relevant resources regarding SuperCollider. This book aspires to be interesting to all seasoned and causal SuperCollider users.

What this book covers

Chapter 1, *Scoping, Plotting, and Metering*, examines basic built-in scoping, plotting, and the metering of waveforms, signals, and numerical datasets in Supercollider. In this chapter, we will discuss how to visualize numerical datasets, signals, and functions; how to scope waveforms and spectra in real time; how to monitor audio levels and numerical data; and how to implement more complex and nonstandard visualizers using various built-in GUI elements.

Chapter 2, *Waveform Synthesis*, elaborates various waveform synthesis techniques, with emphasis on the visual, rather than acoustic, aspects of audio. In this chapter, we will discuss waveform synthesis fundamentals and learn how to generate custom and good-looking (in any subjective way) waveforms based on a series of techniques.

Chapter 3, *Synthesizing Spectra*, is similar in spirit to the *Chapter 2*, *Waveform Synthesis*, yet it deals with spectra rather than with waveforms. In this chapter, we will focus on the visual aspects of audio spectra and learn to synthesize custom and good-looking (again in any subjective way) spectra using a variety of both time-domain and frequency-domain techniques.

Chapter 4, *Vector Graphics*, deals with vector graphics and discusses both fundamental theoretical concepts as well as how to create static drawings of arbitrary complexity in SuperCollider using a wide range of techniques. Color, matrix operations, as well as complex visual structures such as particle systems and fractals are discussed. In this chapter, we will also discuss object modeling with Event and the factory design pattern.

Chapter 5, *Animation*, elaborates on video animation. Therein, we will demonstrate how to implement different kinds of motion, how to create trailing effects, as well as how to animate complex visual structures and systems. We will also introduce ourselves with more advanced techniques, such as emulating environmental forces and real-life systems or designing articulated bodies using kinematics.

Chapter 6, *Data Acquisition and Mapping*, explains how arbitrary real-world numerical data can be retrieved, accessed, processed, and used in SuperCollider, This chapter elaborates on machine listening (that is, how to extract information out of audio signals) and discusses basic mappings and encodings.

Chapter 7, *Advanced Visualizers*, elaborates on a series of advanced examples wherein audio and data are visualized/sonified in various ways. The examples range from trailing waveforms and spectrogram implementations to more imaginative ones featuring kinematic structures, fractals, and particle systems.

Chapter 8, Intelligent Encodings and Automata, serves as an introduction to more advanced topics such as statistical analysis, textual parsing, advanced encodings, neural networks, and cellular automata. Therein we will also discuss a possible implementation of the famous game of life automaton.

Chapter 9, Design Patterns and Methodologies, discusses software architecture and explains how certain design patterns and methodologies can be used by programmers and computer scientists to solve certain recurring problems. Starting with the requirements for a quite complex generative project, we will proceed step-by-step, designing and materializing it in an efficient and conceptually understandable way.

What you need for this book

To use the code provided with this book, you need the latest version of the SuperCollider programming environment, which may be downloaded from `http://supercollider.sourceforge.net/downloads/`. As of this writing, Version 3.6.5 is the official stable release, while 3.7 is still under development. While some of the code heretofore is backward compatible with older versions of the program, the reader is encouraged to use version 3.6.5 or newer. Bear in mind that the GUI part of SuperCollider, on which this book relies a lot, has been substantially changed over the last major updates and, thus, you need to have at least Version 3.5 installed. Other than the SuperCollider programming environment, several examples rely on the SC3-plugins library, which can be downloaded from `http://sourceforge.net/projects/sc3-plugins/`. In some exceptional cases, you will also have to install some `Quark` extensions or even third-party softwares; these are all discussed in the relevant chapters. Yet, you should know how to use the `Quarks` system. Finally, for those examples that depend on a working Internet connection, you should make sure that your computer has access to it.

To make the best of this book, it is both expected and assumed that you are already familiar with the fundamentals of sound synthesis and have some experience with SuperCollider. In particular, you should be comfortable with variables, `SynthDef`/ `Synths`, functions, routines, object-oriented programming, writing classes, scheduling, client/server architecture, and so on. Those readers who are not sure whether their SuperCollider skills are sufficient are encouraged to study the tutorials found on `http://supercollider.sourceforge.net/learning/`.

Who this book is for

This book is for intermediate and advanced SuperCollider users who are interested in mapping and visualization for either scientific or artistic applications. Care has been taken to ensure that the book will be of interest to artists as well as scientists and other specialists, and even to those only indirectly interested in mapping/visualization. The book also discusses a wide range of topics related, but not specific, to the latter, such as automata, generative art, animation, artificial neural networks, and others, and may, therefore, be of interest to anyone having interest in those fields. To some extent, this book is also of interest to all SuperCollider users, including seasoned and new ones because it addresses object modeling and software-architecture-specific topics. Therefore, it provides the necessary background to all those interested in materializing more complex projects of any nature. The primary audience of this book is expected to be artists, scientists, and other specialists interested in mapping, visualization, and generative audiovisual systems.

Conventions

In this book, you will find a number of styles of text that distinguish between different kinds of information. Here are some examples of these styles, and an explanation of their meaning.

Code words in text are shown as follows: "Whenever they are invoked, a parent `Window` is created containing an instance of `Plotter` whose specifics are configured accordingly."

A block of code is set as follows:

```
( // MyfancyStereoScope Example
Server.default.waitForBoot({ // wait for server to boot
  MyFancyStereoScope.new();
  {[Saw.ar(400), Saw.ar(402)]}.play(a)
})
)
```

New terms and **important words** are shown in bold. Words that you see on the screen, in menus or dialog boxes for example, appear in the text like this: "In order to make this code work, we also need to load the `StandardFirmata` code in our Arduino, which we can find in the **Examples | Firmata** submenu of the Arduino **Integrating Development Environment (IDE)**".

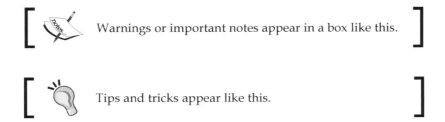

Warnings or important notes appear in a box like this.

Tips and tricks appear like this.

Reader feedback

Feedback from our readers is always welcome. Let us know what you think about this book—what you liked or may have disliked. Reader feedback is important for us to develop titles that you really get the most out of.

To send us general feedback, simply send an e-mail to `feedback@packtpub.com`, and mention the book title via the subject of your message.

If there is a topic that you have expertise in and you are interested in either writing or contributing to a book, see our author guide on `www.packtpub.com/authors`.

Customer support

Now that you are the proud owner of a Packt book, we have a number of things to help you to get the most from your purchase.

Downloading the example code

You can download the example code files for all Packt books you have purchased from your account at `http://www.packtpub.com`. If you purchased this book elsewhere, you can visit `http://www.packtpub.com/support` and register to have the files e-mailed directly to you.

Errata

Although we have taken every care to ensure the accuracy of our content, mistakes do happen. If you find a mistake in one of our books—maybe a mistake in the text or the code—we would be grateful if you would report this to us. By doing so, you can save other readers from frustration and help us improve subsequent versions of this book. If you find any errata, please report them by visiting http://www.packtpub.com/submit-errata, selecting your book, clicking on the **erratasubmissionform** link, and entering the details of your errata. Once your errata are verified, your submission will be accepted and the errata will be uploaded on our website, or added to any list of existing errata, under the Errata section of that title. Any existing errata can be viewed by selecting your title from http://www.packtpub.com/support.

Piracy

Piracy of copyright material on the Internet is an ongoing problem across all media. At Packt, we take the protection of our copyright and licenses very seriously. If you come across any illegal copies of our works, in any form, on the Internet, please provide us with the location address or website name immediately so that we can pursue a remedy.

Please contact us at copyright@packtpub.com with a link to the suspected pirated material.

We appreciate your help in protecting our authors, and our ability to bring you valuable content.

Questions

You can contact us at questions@packtpub.com if you are having a problem with any aspect of the book, and we will do our best to address it.

1
Scoping, Plotting, and Metering

Visualizing audio signals and numerical datasets can be very straightforward in SuperCollider with the built-in scoping, plotting, and metering functionalities. The corresponding GUI objects are simple to use, yet they are highly customizable and extremely powerful. In this chapter we will introduce a series of fundamental techniques, and learn how to design both basic as well as more advanced custom visualizers. However, it should be noted that all the examples herein assume normalized datasets and test signals, deferring the complexities of data mapping and signal optimization to be discussed in depth in subsequent chapters.

The topics that will be covered in this chapter are as follows:

- Plotting audio, numerical datasets, and functions
- Scoping waveforms and spectra
- Metering signals and data
- Nonstandard and complex visualizers

Plotting audio, numerical datasets, and functions

Before discussing how we can scope audio signals in real time, it is worth reviewing the various ways in which we can create static graphs and charts out of arbitrary numerical datasets or signals.

Using plot and plot graph

SuperCollider provides us with a very handy `plot` method. We can use this method in different situations to create graphs on the fly from instances of `Function`, `ArrayedCollection`, `Env`, `Buffer`, `SoundFile`, `WaveTable`, and from a series of other objects (also depending on what extensions we have installed). An example of this is shown in the following code:

```
{SinOsc.ar(100)}.plot(0.1);              // plot a 0.1 seconds of a
sinewave
[5,10,100, 50, 60].plot;                 // plot a numerical dataset
Env([0,1,0],[1,1],[-10,2]).plot;         // plot an envelope
Signal[0,1,0.5,1,0].plot;                // plot a signal
Wavetable.chebyFill(513,[1]).plot;       // plot a wavetable

( // plot the contents of a sound file
Server.default.waitForBoot({ // wait for Server to boot
  Buffer.read(Server.default, Platform.resourceDir +/+
  "sounds/a11wlk01.wav").plot;
});
)
```

In all cases, the resulting graphs will be automatically normalized with respect to the kind of data plotted so that each dimensions' display range is determined by the minimum and maximum quantities it has to represent; that is, to say that the plot's graph is *content-dependent*. Additionally, their meaning depends upon the receiver (that is, the kind of object plotted) so that for instances of `Array`, `Wavetable`, or `Signal`, the graph would represent the value per index; for UGen graphs, amplitude per unit time; for instances of `Env`, value per unit time; and for instances of `Buffer`, amplitude per frame. Since its behavior is different for different kinds of objects, the plot is said to be **polymorphic**. We should always consider the implicit consequences of these two properties. For example, the following two waveforms could be easily mistaken as identical, even if they are not:

```
( // plot two sinusoids of different amplitude
{SinOsc.ar(100)}.plot(bounds:Rect(0,0,400,400));
{SinOsc.ar(100)*2}.plot(bounds:Rect(400,0,400,400));
)
```

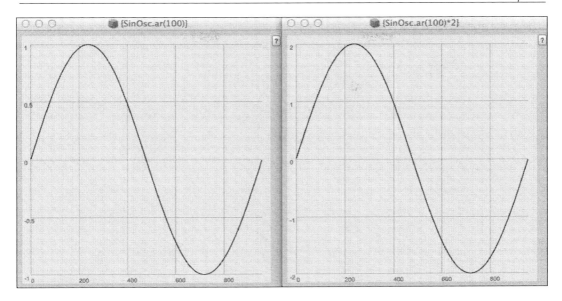

To compensate for such a phenomenon, we need to explicitly set the minima (*minval*) and maxima (*maxval*) arguments. Interestingly enough, we can also plot abstract functions as long as they are one-argument ones and return some arithmetic value. We can do this with the plotGraph method, as follows:

```
{arg x; tan(x**2);}.plotGraph(100,-pi,pi); // graph out of a function
```

Here, the interpreter calculates the output of the given function for 100 different values in the range of ± π and populates the graph with the results; the horizontal axis representing node indexes and the vertical axis representing the function's output.

Buffer objects have a finite capacitance measured in frames; each frame may hold exactly one sample, therefore, a frame is the container of a sample.

Polymorphism in Computer Science refers to the ability in programming to present the same interface for different underlying forms.

Using plotter

Both `plot` and `plotGraph` are convenient methods, which ostensibly are just abstractions of a series of tasks. Whenever they are invoked, a parent `Window` is created containing an instance of `Plotter` whose specifications are configured accordingly. Explicitly creating and using `Plotter` allows sophisticated control over the way our data is plotted. The following code exemplifies a number of features of the `Plotter` object:

```
(  // data visualization using custom plotters
// the parent window
var window = Window.new("Plotter Example", Rect(0,0,640,480)).front;

// the datasets to visualize
var datasetA = Array.fill(1000,{rrand(-1.0,1.0)});// random floats
var datasetB =  [ // a 2-dimensional array of random floats
  Array.fill(10,{rrand(-1.0,1.0)}),
  Array.fill(10,{rrand(-1.0,1.0)})
];

// the plotters
var plotterA = Plotter("PlotterA",Rect(5,5,630,235),window);
var plotterB = Plotter("PlotterB",Rect(5,240,630,235),window);

// setup and customize plotterA
plotterA.value_(datasetA);        // load dataset
plotterA.setProperties(           // customize appearance
  \plotColor, Color.red,          // plot color
  \backgroundColor, Color.black,  // background color
  \gridColorX, Color.white,       // gridX color
  \gridColorY, Color.yellow)      // gridY color
.editMode_(true)    // allow editing with the cursor
.editFunc_({ // this function is evaluated whenever data is edited
  arg plotter,plotIndex,index,val,x,y;
  ("Value: " ++ val ++ " inserted at index: " ++ index ++
    ".").postln;
});

// setup and customize plotterB
plotterB.value_(datasetB);    // load datasetB
plotterB.superpose_(true);    // allow channels overlay
plotterB.setProperties(
```

```
    \plotColor, [Color.blue,Color.green], // plot colors
    \backgroundColor, Color.grey, // background color
    \gridOnX, false,              // no horizontal grid
    \gridOnY, false)              // no vertical grid
  .plotMode_(\steps);            // use step interpolation
  )
```

The result is illustrated in the following screenshot:

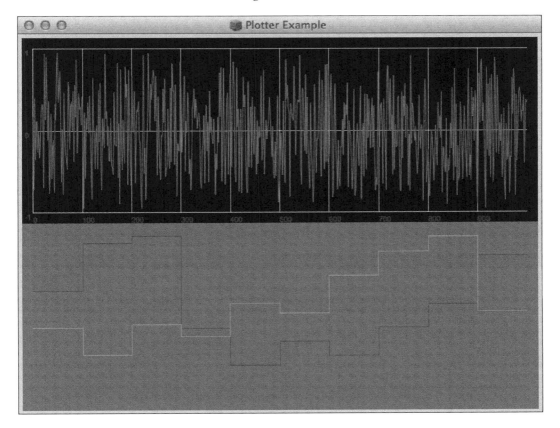

The comments pretty much explain everything. The first `Plotter` object is editable, which means that we can alter the graph when dragging and clicking on it with the mouse. Whenever we do so, `editFunc` will be evaluated with the following that are passed as arguments:

- The `Plotter` object.
- The *plot index* (which is only meaningful if there is more than one graph, such as for multichannel signals, of course).
- The *index position* (horizontal axis value).
- The *value* of the vertical dimension.
- The *x* and the *y* positioning of the cursor.

In this case, while clicking or dragging with the mouse, a simple message is printed in the console.

The second `Plotter` object that operates on a multichannel dataset will create ramps out of every individual channel and superimpose them on the same graph using different colors. Using `plotMode`, we can select between the following alternative data representation modes, namely, `\linear` (linear interpolation), `\points` (data points only), `\plines` (both lines and points), `\levels` (horizontal lines), and `\steps` (ramps).

Using SoundFileView

In a visualization context, we may encounter situations wherein we need to plot the contents of some audio file. We could do so with `Buffer` and `Plotter`, yet there does exist a dedicated class for such cases, namely, `SoundFileView` as shown in the following code:

```
(  // display the contents of a soundfile
// create the view
var view = SoundFileView.new(Window.new("A SoundFileView Example",
640@480).front,640@480);

// load a soundfile in the view using a SoundFile
var file = SoundFile.new;   // create a new SoundFile
file.openRead(Platform.resourceDir +/+ "sounds/a11wlk01.wav");
// read a file
view.soundfile_(file);          // set the soundfile
view.read(0, file.numFrames);   // read the entire soundfile (**for
big soundFiles use .readWithTask instead**)
file.close;     // we no longer need the SoundFile
```

```
// configure appearence
view.timeCursorOn_(false);        // no time cursor
view.gridOn_(false);              // no grid
view.background_(Color.green);    // background color
view.waveColors_([Color.magenta]);
// waveform color (it has to be an array)
)
```

Again the code is pretty straightforward; the only implication being that we need to open and read the actual file with a SoundFile object before we can read its contents into the SoundFileView object. When large sound files are involved, we will have to use readWithTask instead to avoid overloading our computer's memory. Then, if needed, we can use the zoom (or zoomToFrac) and scrollTo methods to only display portions of the file or to animate its contents. For example, the previous code could continue as shown in the following code:

```
// animate the contents of the file
fork{ 100.do { arg counter;
  { // every time we put some GUI-related operation in a Routine we
need to defer it so that it is scheduled in the AppClock instead
    view.zoomToFrac(counter/100); // to total zooming range is 0-1
    view.scrollTo(counter/100); // the total scrolling range is 0-1
  }.defer;
  0.1.wait; // speed of animation
}}
```

Note that SuperCollider will refuse to schedule any GUI-related operation in the SystemClock class, hence we will have to use defer whenever such operations are involved. This is so that we can implicitly schedule them in the AppClock instead.

Scoping signals

Plotter and SoundFileView can be exploited in several ways, but they are not really efficient for scoping real-time audio signals. SuperCollider features dedicated built-in visualizers that we use to easily scope signals in both time and frequency domains.

Scoping waveforms

As far as signals are concerned, we can easily plot their waveforms in real time
by means of simply invoking `scope` on UGen graphs and instances of `Bus` or
`Server`. The `scope` method is a convenient one too, which creates an instance of
`Stethoscope` in the background; the latter being a fully featured virtual oscilloscope.
An example of this is shown in the following code:

```
( // Stethoscope Example
Server.default.waitForBoot({ // wait for server to boot
  {SinOsc.ar}.scope;  // scope a UGen graph
});
)
```

An instance of `Stethoscope` features dedicated controls so that we can configure
its display ranges; select which and how many instances of `Bus` to plot; and switch
between overlay, non-overlay, or Lissajous (that is X/Y) representational modes.
We can design custom oscilloscopes through `ScopeView`, which is a powerful, highly
parameterized waveform visualizer on its own. However, at the time of writing,
and in defiance of `Stethoscope` being fully functional on both kinds of `servers`,
`ScopeView` cooperated only with the internal one. Other than this, its use involves
linking it with a manually allocated instance of `Buffer` whose contents are to be
constantly updated using a `ScopeOut` UGen (and not with an `Out` UGen). In the
following code, we have implemented a custom waveform/phase scope:

```
(  // a custom dual oscilloscope
Server.default = Server.internal;  // make internal the default server
Server.default.waitForBoot({

  var waveScope, phaseScope; // the two scopes

  // allocate two audio buffers
  var bufferA = Buffer.alloc(Server.default, 1024,2);
  var bufferB = Buffer.alloc(Server.default, 1024,2);

  // a stereo signal
  var sound = {
    var signal = Resonz.ar(
      [ ClipNoise.ar(1.7), ClipNoise.ar(1.8) ],
      SinOsc.ar(1000).range(100,500)); // a stereo signal
    ScopeOut.ar(signal, bufferA); // update first buffer
    ScopeOut.ar(signal, bufferB); // update second buffer
    Out.ar(0,signal); // write to output
  }.play;

  // create the main Window
  var window = Window("Dual Oscilloscope", 640@320).front
  .onClose_({ // on close stop sound and free buffers
```

```
    sound.free;
    bufferA.free;
    bufferB.free;
});
window.addFlowLayout; // add a flowLayout to the window

// create the ScopeViews and set their buffers
waveScope = ScopeView(window,314@310).bufnum_(bufferA.bufnum);
phaseScope = ScopeView(window,314@310).bufnum_(bufferB.bufnum);

// customize waveScope
waveScope.style_(1)   // overlay channels
.waveColors_([Color.red,
Color.yellow]).background_(Color.magenta(0.4))
.xZoom_(1.7).yZoom_(1.2);   // scaling factors

// customize phaseScope
phaseScope.style_(2)   // lissajous mode
.waveColors_([Color.magenta]).background_(Color.cyan(0.3))
.xZoom_(1.2).yZoom_(1.2);   // scaling factors
})
)
```

Our custom scope is shown in the following screenshot:

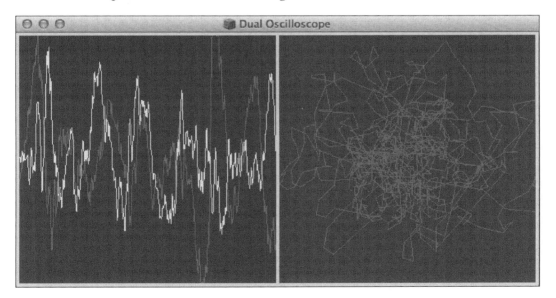

Lissajous curves, named after the 19th century French mathematician Jules Antoine Lissajous, represent the ratio between two different signals and are typically used as phase scopes to visualize the phase differences between the left and right channels of a stereo signal.

Scoping spectra

Frequency domain refers to the representation of signals where the frequency is mapped to the horizontal dimension and amplitude to the vertical dimension. As far as real-time plotting in the frequency domain is concerned, much like waveform scoping, we can either use FreqScope to globally scope the default output of Server; the scopeResponse method to scope UGen graphs on the fly; or the more sophisticated FreqScopeView method to design custom frequency visualizers. Yet, in spite of them being very similar in spirit, there are a couple of major differences between the latter and ScopeView, as illustrated in the following code:

```
(  // a custom Frequency Analyzer
Server.default = Server.local; // set local as the default server
Server.default.waitForBoot({
  // create the parent window
  var window = Window("Frequency Analyzer", 640@480).front
  .onClose_({ // on close
    sound.free;  // stop sound
    scope.kill;  // kill the analyzer
  });

  // the bus to scope
  var bus = Bus.audio(Server.default,2);

  // a stereo signal
  var sound = {
    var signal = Resonz.ar(
      [ ClipNoise.ar(1.7), ClipNoise.ar(1.8) ],
      SinOsc.ar(1000).range(100,500)); // a stereo signal
    Out.ar(bus,signal); // update bus for scoping
    Out.ar(0,signal);   // write to output
  }.play;
```

```
  // the frequency scope
  var scope = FreqScopeView(window,640@480).active_(true);
// activate it
  scope.background_(Color.red).waveColors_([Color.yellow]);
// set colors
  scope.dbRange_(120);  // set amplitude range (in decibels)
  scope.inBus_(bus); // select Bus to scope
})
)
```

Here, we read the signal directly from an instance of Bus, rather than Buffer. Moreover, we have to explicitly set the active variable of FreqScope to true, else no scoping will occur. Ironically enough, as of this writing, FreqScopeView will only collaborate with instances of the localhost Server, thereby making it impossible to have both ScopeView and FreqScopeView based visualizers scoping the very same signal (although we can do so using Stethoscope instead).

Metering levels

Besides plotting the actual signal or dataset, there are situations where we merely want to monitor changes in some magnitude. The most typical scenario is metering the amplitude of some signal, but we could meter anything really, as long as it is represented by some numerical value.

Monitoring signals

Generic metering in SuperCollider is primarily addressed by the LevelIndicator class. To monitor some magnitude specific to a signal, we first need to track it, write the resulting values to some control-rate instance of Bus or to some instance of Buffer, and later use an instance of Routine to manually update the value of LevelIndicator as appropriate. For now, we will limit ourselves to using the Amplitude UGen to only track the amplitude; in *Chapter 6, Data Acquisition and Mapping*, we will discuss how to track other kinds of magnitudes and how to extract information out of audio signals. Note also that a convenient meter method does exist, yet it is only limited to instances of Server and to monitoring the global I/O streams of all its default channels (for example, Server.default.meter).

```
(  // Simple Level Metering
Server.default.waitForBoot({

  // create the parent window
  var window = Window.new("Level Metering", Rect(200,400,60,220)).
  front
```

```
    .onClose_({   // stop routine when the window is closed
      updateIndicator.stop;
      sound.free;
    });

    var bus = Bus.control();    // create a Bus to store amplitude data

    // an audio signal
    var sound = {
      var sound = WhiteNoise.ar(Demand.kr
      (Dust.kr(20),0,Dbrown(0,1,0.3)));
      var amp = Amplitude.kr(sound);  // track the signal's amplitude
      Out.kr(bus, amp);  // write amplitude data to control bus
      Out.ar(0,sound);   // write sound to output bus
    }.play;

    // create and customize Indicator
    var indicator = LevelIndicator(window,Rect(10,10,40,200))
    .warning_(0.5)            // set warning level
    .critical_(0.7)           // set critical level
    .background_(Color.cyan)  // set Color
    .numTicks_(12)            // set number of measurement lines
    .numMajorTicks_(3)        // set number of major measurement lines
    .drawsPeak_(true);        // draw Peak Values

    // update the Indicator's value with a routine
    var updateIndicator = fork{loop{
      bus.get({   // get current value from the bus
        arg value;
        {indicator.value_(value);     // set Indicator's value
          indicator.peakLevel_(value); // set Indicator's peak value
        }.defer(); // schedule in the AppClock
      });
      0.01.wait; // indicator will be updated every 0.01 seconds
    }};
  });
  )
```

Again, note that we use a `defer` block to schedule anything that is GUI-related to the `AppClock` subclass.

Monitoring numerical data

Apart from a signal's magnitude, `LevelIndicator` can be used to monitor any kind of data we may be interested in. In the following code, we loop through an eight-channel multidimensional dataset:

```
(  // Monitoring a complex numerical Dataset
var indicators, updateIndicators;
var index = 0;  // a global index used to iterate through the dataset
var dataset = Array.fill(8,{Array.fill(1000,{rrand(0,1.0)})});
// a multi-dimensional dataset

// create window
var window = Window.new("Monitoring a complex numerical dataset",
360@210).front.onClose_({ updateIndicators.stop });
window.addFlowLayout; // add flowLayout

// create and customize 8 Level indicators
indicators = Array.fill(8, {LevelIndicator(window,40@200)});
indicators.do { arg item;
  item.warning_(0.8).critical_(0.9).background_(Color.cyan).drawsPeak_
(true);
};

// update the indicators with a routine
updateIndicators = fork{loop{
  indicators.do{ arg item, i; {
    var value = dataset[i][index];  // read value from the dataset
    item.value_(value);             // set each Indicator's value
    item.peakLevel_(value);         // set each Indicator's peak value
  }.defer();  // schedule in the AppClock
  };
  // increment index or set to 0 if it has exceeded dataset's size
  if ( index < 1000) {index = index + 1;} {index = 0; };
  0.1.wait; // indicators will be updated every 0.1 seconds
}};
)
```

This time an array of `LevelIndicator` objects is used instead of a singleton element, and of course, there is no need for some specialized tracking UGen. We merely use an instance of `Routine` to access the dataset by means of a global index, which is accordingly incremented once some datum is read. This is so that it always reflects the position of the next object. We will also need an `if` construct to zero out the index once it has exceeded our dataset's size in order to reiterate from the beginning.

Nonstandard and complex visualizers

Having discussed the basic ways in which we can visualize numerical data and audio, we will now demonstrate how we can exploit the built-in GUI elements to implement more complicated or nonstandard visualizers. In particular, we will discuss how we can reappropriate GUI elements originally meant to carry out different tasks, and how to combine the various built-in visualizers in more complex ones.

Nonstandard visualizers

Despite the existence of dedicated objects that cater to all our basic scoping, plotting, and metering needs, the use of simpler and less sophisticated GUI elements is to be considered sometimes because of their characteristic crudeness, which may be just what we are after for certain projects. As in the previous example, we can manually set the value of almost all GUI objects, and that being so, we can exploit them accordingly to design imaginative, uncanny visualizers. For example, we could make the previous code appropriate so that it monitors both the values as well as the distance between any two consecutive adjacent entries in our dataset using `RangeSliders`:

```
updateSliders = fork{loop{
  sliders.do{ arg item, i; {
    var value;
    // store current and previous values in an array and sort it so
    that the smaller number is always the first
    value = [dataset[i][index-1], dataset[i][index]].sort;
    // set each RangeSlider's value
    item.setSpan(value[0],value[1]);
  }.defer; };
  if ( index < 1000) {index = index + 1;} {index = 0; }; // increment
  0.1.wait; // sliders will be updated every 0.1 seconds
}};
```

The entire code can be found online.

A complex scope

After having discussed all major built-in signal visualizers in SuperCollider, it is trivial to combine them in a singleton visualizer. Nonetheless, the server inconsistency of ScopeView and FreqScopeView is an obstacle not easy to surpass. Since it is probably a matter of time before a future version of SuperCollider solves this problem, it does make sense to attempt it, even if only for educational reasons. The code for MyFancyStereoScopeClass is given online. We have to save it onto a file with the .sc extension, copy it into our extensions folder (which can be always retrieved by evaluating Platform.userAppSupportDir), and recompile the SuperCollider's Class library before we can use it as shown in the following code snippet:

```
( // MyfancyStereoScope Example
Server.default.waitForBoot({ // wait for server to boot
  MyFancyStereoScope.new();
  {[Saw.ar(400), Saw.ar(402)]}.play(a)
})
)
```

If all scopes were functional, our custom stereo scope would appear as shown in the following screenshot:

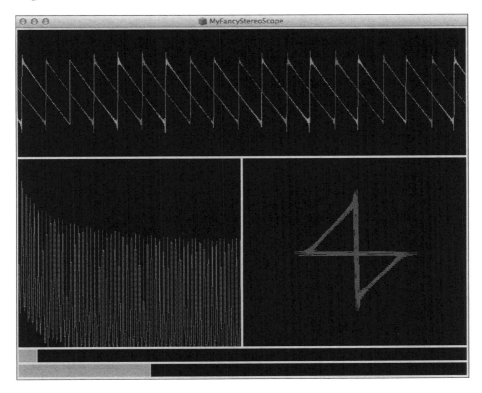

Summary

In this chapter we have learned how to design simple as well as more advanced visualizers in order to plot, scope, or meter audio signals and normalized numerical data in various ways. Hitherto, we have implemented custom spectrum, phase and waveform scopes, signal and dataset plotters, meters, and even nonstandard visualizers using a wide range of objects and methodologies. However, before advancing onto designing even more sophisticated techniques, we need to elaborate on the visual aspects of signals themselves so that they both sound and look interesting enough to scope.

In the next chapter, in particular, we will deal with waveform synthesis and discuss a series of techniques to synthesize appropriate waveforms.

2
Waveform Synthesis

As far as scoping in the time-domain is concerned, we need to be able to optimize our waveforms so that they both look and sound interesting. Subsequently, we will elaborate on a series of techniques to synthesize and manipulate waveforms from a purely visual-oriented perspective. Even if these techniques originate from the realms of traditional audio synthesis or **Digital Signal Processing** (**DSP**), we will use the rather uncanny term waveform synthesis herein to emphasize that our focus is on the visual aspects of audio signals. It has to be noted that in defiance of the abundance of technical handbooks relevant to audio synthesis, waveform synthesis has been largely overlooked hitherto.

The topics that will be covered in this chapter are as follows:

- Waveform synthesis fundamentals
- Custom periodic and aperiodic waveform generators
- Wavetable lookup and wave shaping synthesis
- Unary, binary, and bitwise waveform transformations

Waveform synthesis fundamentals

At this point, it is important to highlight the subtle but fundamental differences between the concepts of *signal*, *waveform*, *sound*, and *audio*. A signal is just a function in the mathematical sense—a stream of information in response to some mutating variable. Sound can be defined as a mechanical pressure wave transmitted through some medium within a certain range of frequencies; technically speaking, sound is not necessarily audible. A wave would be a series of continuous fluctuations of energy through some kind of medium and over the course of time. Audio refers to some sort of electrical or digital representation of sound. Although sound can be represented as audio and audio can be translated into physical sound, these two notions are fundamentally distinct from each other. As the name implies, a waveform is defined as the particular shape and a form of a wave, and by definition it is specific to the time domain.

Time domain representation

Audio is a signal, any kind of sonic representation being a function of some sort. Signals in the time domain are conceptualized as streams of information against the constant flow of time. However, audio signals are not necessarily time-domain specific. In the time domain, digital signals are functions of discrete (that is, not continuous) amplitude values per unit time (measured in samples). A constantly updated graph of these values (typically in the vertical axis) against time is just a visualization of this signal's waveform, which is therefore a time-domain specific representation.

To understand what exactly a waveform represents, consider how audio signals are translated to physical sound and vice versa. To represent physical sonic waves in the digital domain, we first need to convert them into fluctuations of electrical potential (that is, voltage) using some kind of a transducer (for instance, a microphone) and then convert this alternating voltage into a discrete stream of numbers. The latter stage is referred to as sampling and is implemented by simply measuring the amplitude of the voltage at regular time intervals per second (that is, the sampling rate). With the same token, in order to translate a digital signal into an actual sound we need to first convert it into an electrical audio signal, wherein amplitude measurements will be converted to electrical potential (voltage). Then, we can use this electrical signal to drive our speakers' cones in order to stimulate air and create physical waves (that is, sound) whose air pressure is explicitly analogous to that of the original electrical signal.

In other words, the waveform of some signal is just a representation of how air will vibrate when the former is translated to sound, notwithstanding the various losses and artifacts involved. Audio waveforms and their corresponding physical tokens are merely different ways to represent the same information, at least ideally. Yet, our auditory system being fundamentally different than our visual one, certain characteristics of a waveform can only be appreciated in the visual domain and vice versa. The two signals in the following screenshot are identical sounds even if their waveforms are distinctly different:

```
( // two different waveforms that sound identical
  {[    Mix.new(SinOsc.ar((1..10)*200,pi,1/(1..10))*0.2), // left
        Mix.new(SinOsc.ar((1..10)*200,pi/2,1/(1..10))*0.2) // right
  ]}.scope;
)
```

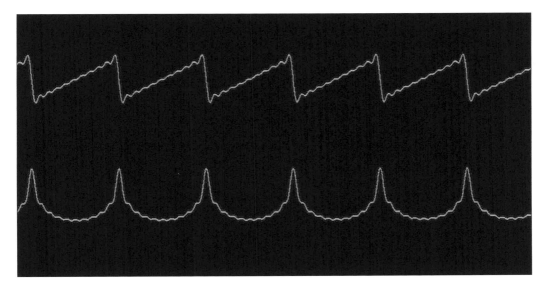

Waveform species

Largely speaking, there are two main families of waveforms: periodic and aperiodic. As the name implies, **periodic waveforms** comprise of repetitive patterns and thus we can speak of *wavelength* (that is, the distance over which the waveform repeats itself), *frequency* (the number of such repetitions per second), and *period* (the time it takes to complete one vibrational cycle). Such waveforms exhibit a definite sense of *pitch* (that is, perceived tonality) and typically, a number of distinct *overtones* (that is, secondary frequencies) that may be *harmonically* (that is, being an integer multiple of) or even *inharmonically* related to the fundamental frequency. **Aperiodic waveforms**, as the name implies, do not consist of repeating patterns, at least as far as human perception is concerned. Therefore, we can no longer speak of frequency, wavelength, or period; but rather, we can speak about sounds of indefinite pitch characterized by the presence of energy in broad frequency ranges. These types of sounds are sometimes referred to as *noises*. Other kinds of waveforms do exist. However, they can be easily conceptualized as either having a quasi-(a)periodic behavior over the course of time or of being an aggregate of several simpler ones.

To some extent, just by looking at the waveform we can safely make assumptions about its sonic characteristics. As far as periodic waveforms are concerned, there is a direct analogy between wavelength and frequency. Thus, just by looking at the waveform we can have a rough idea of what its fundamental frequency can be. Furthermore, we can also have an idea about their harmonic content: waveforms that have a sawtooth like shape feature both even and odd harmonics; triangular ones featuring only odd harmonics, and sinusoidal ones featuring none. In general, the presence of straight-line segments or abrupt corners and ramps denotes the presence of several (theoretically infinite) frequency coefficients that span in the upper-frequency range. By the same token, the presence of continuous mellow curves denotes the presence of just a few frequency coefficients, usually harmonically related partials. Since the human auditory perception is only limited to a certain range of frequencies and since audio reproduction equipment is designed to only handle such kind of frequencies, it does make sense to limit the output of certain generators within this range only. Such kind of generators are called band-limited generators. Their waveforms can be dramatically different from their non band-limited equivalents, especially at high frequencies, as the former will typically smooth out all straight-line and ramped segments. For example:

```
{[ LFSaw.ar(1000), Saw.ar(1000) ]}.scope(zoom:5.9);
// non band limited vs. band-limited versions of the same waveform
```

Note that audio reproduction equipment, including converters, amplifiers, and crossovers, are not designed to handle signals with energy outside a certain frequency range and the speakers' cones cannot physically move instantly between discontinuous positions to properly reproduce non band-limited waveforms featuring rectangular segments. Attempting to do so will always result in nasty artifacts such as aliasing distortion. Hence, we should be extremely cautious with such signals in order to avoid damaging our speakers or (worst) our ears. Other than this, SuperCollider has a plentitude of generators already implemented for all standard and several nonstandard types of both periodic and aperiodic waveforms, which we assume to be already known to the reader.

> **Aliasing distortion** occurs when the sampling rate is not high enough to properly represent high-register frequencies. The latter will characteristically fold into lower registers and produce undesired artifacts.

DC, amplitude, frequency, and phase

The term DC (direct current) originates from the world of analogue signal processing and denotes the presence of static voltage applied to some signal. Of course, in SuperCollider we do not directly deal with electrical signals; yet, there is a digital equivalent that will result in actual static voltage when audio is sent to our hardware's output. The presence of dc offset displaces the waveform upwards (or downwards for a negative offset) in the vertical dimension. We can easily achieve this in SuperCollider if we add a nonzero constant to a signal, either using the + binary operator or using the add parameter present in almost all UGens. Note that the DC offset is not audible per se; nevertheless, it may result in clipping distortion and poor audio performance because we limit the range within which the speakers' cone will move. It can even cause damage to our equipment if the actual electrical DC offset is high enough. Therefore, if we want to bias our waveform without any of these side effects, we have to prepare different versions of our waveform for scoping and sonification, respectively. Note that this is an invaluable technique to remember. In the following code we demonstrate how to do this using a secondary audio Bus object, as well as how to remove unwanted DC using the LeakDC UGen:

```
(  // safely scoping a DC biased waveform
var bus = Bus.audio;                // an audio bus
{ var sound = Saw.ar(add:0.5,mul:0.5); // dc-biased source
  Out.ar(bus,sound);    // write to bus
  Out.ar(0,LeakDC.ar(sound)); // remove dc and write to output
}.play;
bus.scope;  // scope bus
)
```

Apart from modifying a waveform's vertical positioning, we can also tweak its vertical span or range of deviation by means of modulating their overall amplitude. We can do this by simply multiplying them with a constant number using either the `mul` parameter or the * binary operator. However, in this case, changes are no longer inaudible as they will result in more or less loud signals. Nevertheless, the output waveform will always be a linear function of the input unless we exceed the nominal ± 1 range, in the sense that their overall shape (and therefore, their harmonic content) will be analogous. To modify a waveform's horizontal span, we can simply alter their frequency — be it for periodical ones with lower frequencies resulting in sparser waveforms and higher frequencies resulting in denser waveforms. Note that as far as scoping is concerned, we can also control the vertical or horizontal span of a waveform without affecting it by simply tweaking the zoom variables of `ScopeView`.

The equivalent of DC offset in the horizontal axis is the so-called phase offset, or simply phase. The term is only meaningful for periodic waveforms and refers to the initial angle of a waveform in its origin. In other words, it signifies a waveform will start from a particular point of its vibrational cycle. Phase is measured either in degrees (0 to 360) or radians (2 times π equals 360 degrees), with the latter being the norm in most cases. Phase differences are largely inaudible per se, as exemplified earlier in this chapter wherein two different waveforms sound identical and their only difference was their phase offsets. To modify the phase of some waveform, we can simply use the appropriate argument of its generator (if existent) or slightly delay the signal (if not). To calculate the delay time for a phase difference of *n* radians, first we need to calculate the period of the signal (which is just the reciprocal of frequency), then divide it with 2 times π and multiply it with *n*. For example:

```
{[Saw.ar(500), DelayN.ar(Saw.ar(500),0.1,0.001);]}.scope(zoom:8);
// adding phase offset
```

Note that modulating frequency, amplitude, DC bias, and phase of a waveform will not only result in different visual characteristics in the short run, but more importantly, it will dramatically affect how subsequent waveshaping operations will transform them. This will be discussed later in this chapter.

 Clipping distortion occurs whenever an amplifier or converter is overdriven and attempts to deliver an output voltage beyond its maximum capability.

Custom waveform generators

SuperCollider already provides us a plethora of both basic and more sophisticated waveform generators, and more are available through extension libraries and Quarks. Yet, it also provides us the means to generate our own custom-looking ones, as we will see in this section.

Wavetable lookup synthesis

The famous **wavetable lookup synthesis** technique can be summarized as a repeated reading of a custom *wavetable* (that is, the desired waveform's cycle) according to a given frequency. Apparently we are talking about periodic waveforms, and actually this is the standard methodology in the underlying implementation of most standard oscillators. To perform custom wavetable lookup synthesis, we need to populate an instance of Buffer with the desired wave-cycle and then use Osc (or one of its other flavors: OscN, VOsc, VOSC3, and COsc), as shown in the following code:

```
( // Simple Wavetable Lookup
var buffer = Buffer.alloc(Server.default, 256, 1);
// allocate a Buffer
buffer.sine1([1,0.8,0.1,0.6,0.9], true, asWavetable:true);
// fill it with a wavecycle
{Osc.ar(buffer,500,mul:0.2)}.scope(zoom:2);   // create the waveform
)
```

Note that `Osc` will only collaborate with `Buffer` objects having a size equal to some power of two (at least, as of Version 3.7). In this example, we used the `sine1` method to fill the buffer with values. The `Buffer` class provides us with a number of dedicated methods that we can use to fill it with the sinusoidal coefficients (`sine1`, `sine2`, or `sine3`) or **Chebyshev polynomials** (named after *Pafnuty Chebyshev*, these are a family of orthogonal polynomials). However, note that `asWavetable` has to be set to true for `OSC` to properly read the `Buffer` object. We could also fill the instance of `Buffer` using `Wavetable`, or a `Signal` object instead, relying on the latter's `asWavetable` method. `Signal` has a sophisticated filling (for example, `*hanningWindow`, `*hammingWindow`, `*welchWindow`, `*rectWindow`) as well as data processing (for example, `invert`, `reverse`, `normalize`, `fade`, `overdub`) functionality compared to `Wavetable`. It also features a very useful `fill` method we can use with custom functions. However, there is an important caveat that `asWavetable` will return an instance of `Wavetable` having twice the size of the original `Signal` object. For example, consider the following code:

```
( // using Signals to populate a Buffer
var signal = Signal.fill(256,{1.0.bilinrand})
// fill a signal with the results of a custom function
.overDub(Signal.hanningWindow(256)).invert;
// blend it with a Hanning window and invert it
var waveTable = signal.asWavetable;  // convert it to a WaveTable
var buffer = Buffer.loadCollection(Server.default, waveTable);
// load it to a newly allocated buffer
buffer.plot;  // plot the Buffer's contents
waveTable.size.postln;
// notice that the size is now twice the signal's
)
```

Another slightly more involved instance wherein we use an editable `Plotter` method to dynamically draw our wavetable in real time is shown in the following code:

```
( // Wavetable-lookup using an editable Plotter
Server.default.waitForBoot({
  var buffer = Buffer.alloc(Server.default, 512); // allocate Buffer
  var plotter = Plotter.new("Wavetable", 800@300)
// create the Plotter
  .value_(0!256).editMode_(true).editFunc_({ arg plotter;
    var signal = plotter.value.as(Signal); // convert Array to Signal
    var wavetable = signal.asWavetable;
// convert signal to a wavetable
    buffer.sendCollection(wavetable,0); // send to Buffer
  });
  {Out.ar(0,Osc.ar(buffer,250))}.scope(zoom:1.8);
// wavetable lookup synthesis
})
)
```

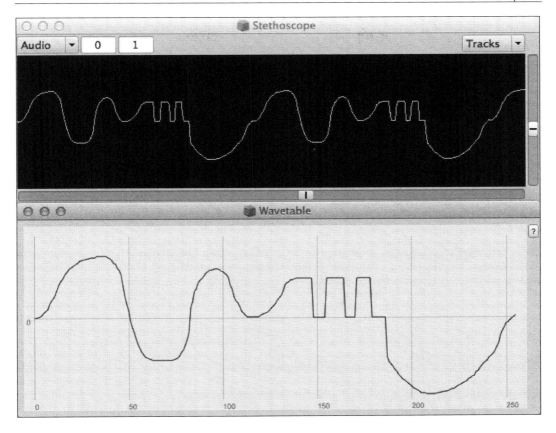

Using envelopes as wavetables

We can also realize wavetable lookup synthesis or at least a series of conceptually similar techniques without resorting to specialized UGens such as osc. Sometimes it proves easier and more efficient to just deviate rather than rely on the available filling methods to create the desired wave cycle. Consider the following code wherein we use EnvGen to have an Env object periodically repeated:

```
(
// custom waveform using envelope generator
{   var freq = 150, env;   // frequency and envelope
  // create the envelope and use circle to make it a repeating one
  env = Env([-1,1,1,0,-1],[1.5,0.5,1,0.5].normalizeSum,[0,0,-4,1]).
circle;
  EnvGen.ar(env,timeScale:freq.reciprocal) * 0.8;
  // oscillate at given frequency
}.scope();
)
```

This example is more of a hack really, since envelope generators are not supposed to be used for these sort of things, yet it proves less involved and more efficient in this particular case. Instead of first creating a `Signal` or `Wavetable` object (which would be quite involved for this particular wavecycle anyway) and loading it into an instance of `Buffer`, we simply used an instance of `Env` to describe our wave cycle in terms of amplitude, time, and curvature coefficients. For certain shapes, this approach may prove more straightforward and accurate, letting aside that we save a couple of lines of code. Then, invoking the `circle` method guarantees that `EnvGen` will endlessly repeat this envelope to create a periodic waveform. A subtle detail is that we invoked `normalizeSum` on the array with the time values; this will update all entries so that their total sum is one, keeping their individual proportions intact. In this way, we significantly simplify our subsequent calculations so that we can realize any desired frequency now by simply setting `timeScale` to its reciprocal.

Custom aperiodic waveform generators

We need a different strategy to generate custom aperiodic waveforms as the question is no longer how to repeat a well predefined wave cycle, but how to dynamically compute an ever-changing waveform in real time. Fortunately, there are ways to design complex stochastic algorithms easily and efficiently that completely rely on server-side computations. For instance, by means of exploiting the so-called demand rate UGens, as in the following simplistic example:

```
// simplistic Demand rate aperiodic waveform
{Demand.ar(Dust.ar(4000), 0, Dbrown(-1,1,0.1,inf))}.scope;
```

`Demand`, as the name implies, demands the next value from a list of demand rate UGens every time a trigger is received. *Triggers*, in a DSP context are transitions from nonpositive value or zero to a positive one. Herein, we simply demand approximately 4000 amplitude values (in the range of ± 1 and with maximum possible deviation of 0.1 between adjacent values) per second from a demand rate Brownian movement number generator (`Dbrown`). Ostensibly, demand rate UGens are just server-side implementations of patterns. If browsing through the list of available demand rate UGens, we will find all sorts of deterministic, stochastic, or probabilistic number generators and even more complicated generators, such as finite state machines or microprocessor simulations. In the next example, we will use a finite state Markov chain machine (`Dfsm`) to create a more complex aperiodic waveform generator. Herein, we start from 0 and proceed by selecting random states out of a list of possible ones as shown in the following code snippet:

```
( // aperiodic generator based on a demand rate finite state machine
Server.default = Server.internal.waitForBoot({
  { Demand.ar(Impulse.ar(4000), 0, Dfsm([[0], // start at step 0
    Dbrown(-1,1,0.1,4),[0,1],
```

```
/* step 0: generate 4 random values (brownian distribution) and then
go to step 0 or step 1 */
    -1,[0,1,2],
// step 1: generate -1 and go to step 0 or to step 1 or to step 2
    Dseq([-0.2,-0.4,-0.8],6),[0,3],
/* step 2: generate 6 sequences of -0.2,-0.4,-0.8 and then go to
either step 0 or to step 3 */
    Dwhite(-0.5,1,10),[2]
/* step: 3 generate 10 random values in the -0.5,1 range then go to
step 2 */
  ]));
  }.scope(zoom:3);
})
)
```

Note that the `Dfsm` class is not available in the standard SuperCollider distribution, but through the SC3Plugins bundle which can be downloaded from `http://sourceforge.net/projects/sc3-plugins/`

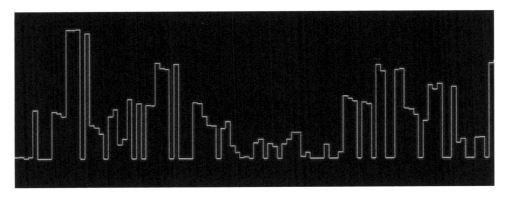

 Markov chains, named after the 19th–20th century Russian mathematician *Andrei Markov*, refer to mathematical systems that undergo transitions between a finite number of possible states and with respect to a set of instructions.

Waveform transformations

Synthesizing custom-looking waveforms from scratch is an invaluable tool. Still, there are certain kinds of waveforms that are easier to generate by means of manipulating other ones, and there are cases wherein we are merely interested in optimizing or appropriating some existent audio signals. The last part of this chapter is dedicated to all sorts of waveform transformation techniques, again with an explicit emphasis on how they will affect the shape, rather than the sound of a signal.

Waveshaping

Waveshaping stands for transforming a waveform with respect to some transfer function. Basic waveshaping can be performed using `Clip`, `Fold`, `Wrap` UGens, or their equivalent convenient methods (`clip`, `fold` and `wrap`, respectively):

```
// convenient waveshaping
{SinOsc.ar(300).clip(-0.5,0.5)}.scope;  // clipping output to +-0.5
{SinOsc.ar(300).fold(-0.5,0.5)}.scope;  // folding output to +-0.5
{SinOsc.ar(300).wrap(-0.5,0.5)}.scope;  // wrapping output to +-0.5
```

In the following figure, we can see how the original waveform is transformed in each case:

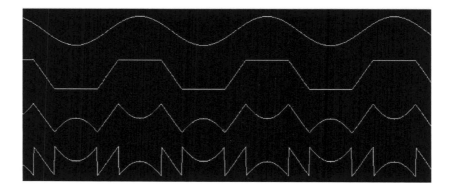

Only the part of the input waveform that lies outside the given bounds (± 0.5 herein) will be affected. Values within this range will remain unchanged, while values outside it will be either truncated (`clip`), folded back (`fold`), or wrapped (`wrap`) onto the valid range by means of a simple mathematical formulae. Waveshaping epitomizes how subtle variations in the amplitude or DC offset or the original signal may result in dramatically different waveforms. For instance, consider the result if we simply amplify or bias the previous signals:

```
// waveshaping and amplitude/dc-offset
{LeakDC.ar(SinOsc.ar(300,add:1).clip(-0.5,0.5))}.scope;
// clipping output between -0.5,0.5
{SinOsc.ar(300,mul:4).fold(-0.5,0.5)}.scope;     // folding output
between -0.5,0.5
{LeakDC.ar(SinOsc.ar(300,mul:4, add:2).wrap(-0.5,0.5))}.scope;
// wrapping output between -0.5,0.5
```

The new waveforms are illustrated in the following screenshot:

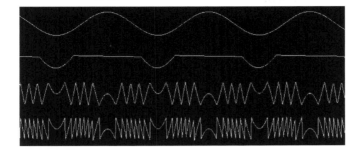

By using envelopes we could dynamically control the intensity of waveshaping by defining specific amplitude and DC offset trajectories over the course of time. Remember that we can always use LeakDC to compensate for the presence of undesired DC before sending our signal to the audio output.

Returning to the notion of a transfer function, let us try to understand what it stands for practically. For example, in the case of clip, we could describe it as shown in the following code snippet:

```
{arg in, min, max;
   if (in <= min)      // if lesser or equal than min
   {min}               // then min
   { if (in >= max)    // else, if in greater or equal than max
     {max}             // then max
     {in}              // then in
   }
}
```

The corresponding graph (for min -0.5 and max 0.5) for this is shown in the following figure:

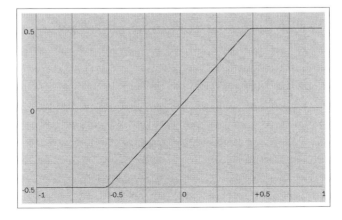

This graph describes in visual terms what we may expect in the output for a given input, mapping every individual amplitude value of the input to another. Using the `Shaper` UGen we can achieve sophisticated waveshapers by means of providing our own custom transfer functions as instances of `Wavetable` containing analogous graphical representations. For example:

```
( // Custom waveshaping example
/* allocate and fill the Buffer with a wavetable of sinusoidal
coefficients */
var buffer = Buffer.alloc(Server.default, 512).sine1([0.1,0.6,1,0.5],
true,true);
{ Shaper.ar(buffer, SinOsc.ar(300,mul:3,add:1))*0.3}.scope;
// waveshaping
)
```

Unary operations

In SuperCollider, we can easily perform certain waveform transformations by means of simple operations. Most of these operations are essentially just flavors of waveshaping; yet, it is a lot easier to conceptualize and predict their output if we simply think of them in terms of their corresponding mathematical operations. In particular, unary (that is, with no argument other than the input waveform) operations are not parameterized per se, and thus are even simpler to conceive. A nonexhaustive list of the most interesting unary operations classified in categories are explained as follows:

- **Polarity operations**: These operations involve the `abs` (absolute value) and `sign` operator (`-1` if input is lower than 0, `0` if the input is 0, and `1` if the input is larger than 0). These operators will change the input waveform on the account of its polarity. The `abs` operator is typically used to rectify waveforms and `sign` to create rectangular waves with respect to the input's polar characteristics.

- **Logarithmic and exponential operations**: These operations involve `squared` (input's square), `cubed` (input's cube), `exp` (Euler's number raised to the input), `log` (natural logarithm), `log2` (base 2 logarithm),and `log10` (base 10 logarithm). Note that definitions of `squared` and `cubed` have been extended to also result in bipolar waveforms (that is, having both positive and negative parts) if the input is bipolar. Also, all logarithmic operators will generate only negative unipolar waveforms (that is, having only a negative part), when the input is in the nominal ±1 amplitude range.

- **Trigonometric operations**: These operations involve sin (sine), cos (cosine), tan (tangent), asin (arcsine), acos (arccosine), atan (arctangent), sinh (hyperbolic sine), cosh (hyperbolic cosine), and tanh (hyperbolic tangent). Note that cos, acos, and cosh will all result in DC-biased waveforms.

- **Clipping operations**: These operations involve floor (next lower integer), ceil (next higher integer), distort (S-shaped waveshaper), softclip (such as distort, but with a linear ± 0.5 segment). floor and ceil will always generate rectangular waves of positive polarity if the original waveform is in the nominal ±1 amplitude range.

- **Miscellaneous mathematical operations**: These operations involve sqrt (square root, the definition is extended to also result in bipolar waveforms) and reciprocal (the reciprocal of the input). Note that in reciprocal's case, when the input crosses zero the result will be infinity, which in a waveform's context will result in distortion. We have to DC bias the original accordingly to compensate for this.

The following code demonstrates unary operations in action (compare left to right channels):

```
// examples of unary operations
{[ LFSaw.ar(200), LFSaw.ar(200).abs]*0.8}.scope; // rectify waveform
{[ LFTri.ar(200), LeakDC.ar(LFTri.ar(200).cos)]*0.8}.scope;
// convert triangular to rectified sinusoid
{[ SinOsc.ar(200), SinOsc.ar(200).floor]*0.8}.scope;
// next height integer
{[ SinOsc.ar(200), SinOsc.ar(200,mul:2).floor * 0.5 ]*0.8}.scope;
// the same on an amplified sine wave
{[SinOsc.ar(200),SinOsc.ar(200).sign]*0.8}.scope;
// convert a sine into a rectangular wave
{[SinOsc.ar(),LeakDC.ar(SinOsc.ar(add:2).reciprocal)]}.scope;
/* reciprocal of a sine wave, dc-bias is needed to avoid infinities
when the input crosses zero */
```

Binary operations

SuperCollider also features a series of useful binary (that is, having two operands, hereinafter referred to as *a* and *b*) operators that we can apply on waveforms. A nonexhaustive list of the most interesting binary operations classified in categories are given as follows:

- **Simple mathematical operations**: This operation includes + (addition), - (subtraction), * (multiplication), / (division), % (modulo), ** (exponentiation, extended for signals to also result in bipolar waveforms if the input is bipolar), and pow (standard exponentiation). Note that we have to be careful with / as it will produce infinity when the denominator is zero — DC biasing is a plausible way to compensate.

- **Quantization operations**: The round operator rounds *a* to the nearest multiple of *b*, and the trunc operator truncates *a* to the nearest multiple of *b*. They are very useful operations that we can use to convert curvatures in a waveform into zigzags.

- **Mathematical operations**: The hypot (square root of the sum of the squares of *a* and *b*), hypotApx (an approximation of hypot), atan2 (arctangent of *b*/*a*), sumsqr (sum of squares), difsqr (difference of squares), sqrsum (square of the sum), sqrdif (square of the difference), and absdif (absolute value of the difference) are operators that are typically used to combine two different waveforms with each other.

- **Clipping operations**: The min (clips amplitudes above *b*), max (clips amplitudes below *b*), thresh (0 when *a* < *b*, otherwise *a*), amclip (0 when *b* <= 0, *a**b when *b* > 0), scaleneg (*a**b when *a* < 0, otherwise a), clip2 (clips to ± *b*), wrap2 (wraps to ± *b*), fold2 (folds to ±*b*), and excess (residual of clipping).

- **Comparison operations**: The < (lesser than), > (greater than), <= (lesser or equal than), >= (greater or equal than) are operators that will generate a zero when the comparison is false and one when the comparison is true. Hence, we can use them to convert the input into a rectangular waveform of some sort, upon some condition of arbitrary complexity.

It may take some time to really master binary operators as they foster a more mathematical way of thinking about waveforms. Yet, as exemplified in the following examples, they are capable of imaginative transformations by very simple means:

```
// examples of binary operations
{SinOsc.ar(100).excess(0.5)}.scope;
// the residual of clipping of a sine wave
{WhiteNoise.ar(0.4).amclip(SinOsc.ar(100))}.scope;
// create whitenoise pulses
```

```
{SinOsc.ar(100).thresh(SinOsc.ar())}.scope;
// threshold a sine wave with respect to another
{LFNoise2.ar(400).scaleneg(LFSaw.ar(1000))}.scope;
/* Ring modulation between LFSaw and LFnoise only when LFNoise2's
polarity is negative */
{LeakDC.ar(SinOsc.ar(300) < WhiteNoise.ar())}.scope;
/* compare a sine wave with white noise to generate a weird
rectangular wave */
```

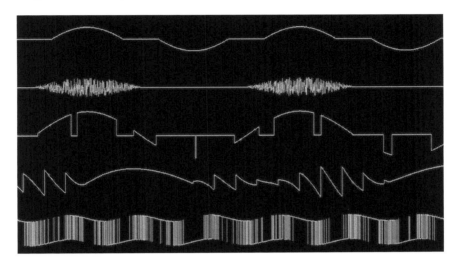

Bitwise operations

SuperCollider also supports bitwise logic and bit shifting operations on audio signals, namely: & (bitwise and), | (bitwise or), not (bitwise not), bitXor (bitwise exclusive or), << (binary shift-left), and >> (binary shift-right). **Bitwise operations** are techniques fundamental to low-level computing and to the architecture of hardware processors themselves. Fundamentally, they are primitive ways to manipulate binary numerals at the level of their individual bit patterns.

For instance, & will return 1 only if both of its operands are 1, | will return 1 if at least of its operands is 1, and so on. In particular, and as far as audio signals are concerned, the & operator will return 1 if the absolute values of both its operands are greater or equal to 1 and at least one of them is a positive value, -1 if they are both smaller or equal to -1, and 0 in all other cases. The | operator will return 1 if at least one of its operands is greater or equal to 1, -1 if at least one of its operators is equal or lesser than -1, and 0 in all other cases. The bitXor operator is very similar to |, the only difference being that it generates 0 if both operands' absolute values are greater or equal to 1. The not operator is unary and will return 1 when the input is negative and 0 when the input is positive.

Bit-shifting operators are a bit idiosyncratic, especially for signals. The << and >> operators will shift the bit pattern of the *left* operand to the left or to the right, respectively, by as many digits as instructed by the value of the *right* operand. For decimal numbers, we can think of these operations as multiplying the *left* operand with the power of 2 of the *right* operand in the case of the << operand (for instance, 3 << 3 results into 3 * (2**3), that is, 24) and as dividing with the power of 2 of the *right* operand in the case of the >> operand (for instance, 24 >> 3 equals 24 / (2**3), that is, 3). As far as signals are concerned, bit shifting operations are only meaningful with integer values and will truncate their operands' values to the nearest integer. Therefore, in order to have any serious effects on our waveforms, we have to resort to the common trick of DC-biasing or amplifying our signals before the operation—but this time we will probably have to be more extreme. Due to the nature of the bitwise operations all the resulted waveforms will consist of straight-line and rectangular segments. Nonetheless, these operations are very useful as they can sculpt waveforms in ways that are almost impossible to achieve otherwise.

Consider the following examples:

```
// bitwise operations on waveforms
{(SinOsc.ar(mul:1.2) | WhiteNoise.ar(mul:1.2))*0.7}.scope;
// complex waveform from two basic ones
{(LeakDC.ar(LFSaw.ar(mul:4,add:2) << 3) >> 1) * 0.1}.scope;
// sculpt a sawtooth wave using bit-shifting
{(LeakDC.ar( SinOsc.ar(mul:4,add:2) << WhiteNoise.ar(2,2)) >> 3) *
0.2}.scope; // generate complex shapes using bit-shifting
```

The resulting waveforms are shown in the following image:

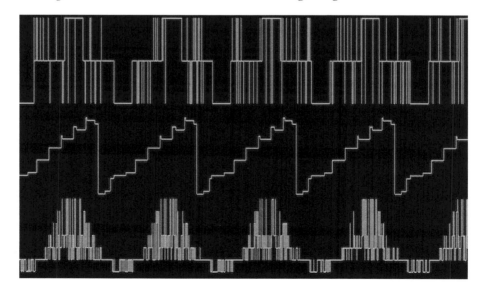

Summary

In this chapter, we discussed time domain audio representation and we elaborated on various ways to synthesize and manipulate signals to achieve imaginative waveforms. These included standard waveshaping and wavetable lookup techniques, as well as less the common ones such as bitwise transformations, demand rate based stochastic generators or envelope-based oscillators.

In the next chapter, we will pinpoint the frequency domain and examine techniques to synthesize and process spectra — the equivalent of waveforms in the frequency-domain.

3
Synthesizing Spectra

Audio signals are usually dealt with either as functions of time or as functions of frequency. In the previous chapter, we discussed time-domain audio representation and elaborated on various ways in which we can synthesize and manipulate waveforms. Likewise, now we will discuss frequency-domain audio representation and elaborate on the various techniques we can use to synthesize or manipulate spectra (the equivalents of waveforms in the frequency domain). Again, we will be primarily concerned with their visual aspects rather than with their acoustic properties, as there is already a plentitude of technical resources relevant to the latter, which is available to the reader.

The topics that will be covered in this chapter are as follows:

- Frequency-domain fundamentals
- Fast Fourier Transform (FFT) in SuperCollider
- Synthesizing new spectra
- Transforming the existing spectra
- Optimizing spectra for scoping

Introducing the frequency domain

The frequency domain is nothing more than an alternative way to represent some signal. Nevertheless, it is of fundamental importance as it visualizes certain kinds of information that cannot be appreciated otherwise.

Spectra

Signals in the frequency-domain are represented as functions of amplitude (vertical axis) versus frequency (horizontal axis). As such, a spectrum is fundamentally different from a waveform in that it represents how sound manifests in perceptual, rather than physical space. Indeed, spectra give no indication on how a signal would manifest in the physical world if translated to sound, yet they do accurately describe what the harmonic content of this sound would be. This should be of no surprise if we are familiar with the mechanics of hearing and particularly, of the physiology of the inner ear. Therein, a number of hearing cells inside the basilar membrane, each of which is sensitive to a particular frequency range, will fire neural spikes when stimulated. That is to say that the inner ear performs some sort of spectral analysis to inform the brain of a sound's harmonic content. Leaving cognition aside, we largely perceive sound as a time-varying spectrum. Despite some superficial analogies, spectra and waveforms are very different beings and subsequently, it is not very helpful to think of one in terms of the other. Their visual characteristics stand for completely different kinds of information.

In a very similar fashion to our auditory apparatus, we can analyze a time-domain signal according to a bank of fixed frequency ranges (the so-called *bins*) in order to represent it in the frequency-domain. Before being able to listen to such a signal, of course, we have to first synthesize a waveform out of it, that is, convert it back into the time-domain. From the plethora of algorithms that implement spectral analysis, the most important is unanimously the **Fast Fourier Transform** (FFT). *Jean Baptiste Joseph Fourier* was an 18th-19th century French mathematician who claimed that any kind of continuous periodic signal, however complex it may be, can be accurately represented as a sum of arbitrary sinusoid and cosine waves. Today, after his ideas have been thoroughly refined and evolved, we can rely on FFT to accurately model any kind of signal as a sum of partials (that is, frequency coefficients) that can be optimized to be fast enough for real-time applications.

> The basilar membrane is a stiff membrane within the cochlea of the inner ear, which separates two liquid-filled organs (the scala media and the scala tympani) and that is also the base for the sensory cells of human hearing.

Fast Fourier Transform in SuperCollider

A formal discussion of FFT would be far beyond the scope of this book; it suffices to say that the FFT algorithm analyzes temporal snapshots of our signal in order to generate a time-varying spectrum. Nonetheless, it has to be said that FFT is not a transparent process; there are several caveats to consider, the most important being a trade-off between spectral resolution and accurate timing: the greater the first, the less accurate the second, and vice versa. Technically speaking, a spectrum is usually represented in either *Cartesian* (complex) or *Polar* form. These two forms are merely different ways to represent the same information, yet they can be conceptualized differently. In its complex flavor, the signal represents the amplitudes of the cosine coefficients (real part) and the amplitudes of the sine coefficients (imaginary part) that would synthesize the original signal if added together. Since cosine signals are essentially just sinusoid ones with their phase shifted by π radians, we can easily think of the polar representation as consisting of the magnitudes of the bins and their phase offsets.

In SuperCollider, both the FFT as well as the inverted FFT (that is, to synthesize a time-domain signal out of a spectrum) are implemented, namely the FFT and the IFFT UGens. FFT will analyze the time-domain signals and store that data inside an instance of Buffer (we typically use LocalBuf for convenience) and return an FFT chain. Note that the size of the Buffer object has to be a power of two and a multiple of SuperCollider's block size; typical sizes are 512, 1024, 2048, and 4096. The resolution of the spectral analysis (the number of bins) depends on the size of our Buffer object; bear in mind, however, that as already mentioned, the greater the size, the slower the analysis and thus, the lesser the time-accuracy. A singleton FFT buffer will hold both the magnitudes and the phases, so for each of these measurements only half of its size is available, yet there is no real information loss, since the output of an FFT analysis for digital signals is made of two halves, mirrored at half of the sampling frequency. Note also that for multichannel signals, we need to provide an appropriate array of Buffer objects (and not a multichannel one). Then, having switched to the frequency domain, we can chain up instances of the various available phase-vocoder (identified by the PV_ prefix) UGens to manipulate and process spectra. These UGens will convert, as needed, between Cartesian and polar representations, making it impossible to know in which form the values will be at any given time. Finally, when we are done processing in the frequency domain, we can use the IFFT UGen to synthesize a time-domain signal out of the FFT chain.

Nevertheless, we do not necessarily have to rely on frequency-domain techniques to synthesize spectra; we can do so by relying solely on time-domain techniques as will soon be demonstrated. Yet, in order to have some spectrum visualized, we do need to perform some kind of spectral analysis (which is usually part of the visualizer's very implementation as is the case with `FreqScope`). This implies that our visualization will suffer FFT artifacts even if our audio signal does not. We will discuss ways to compensate for this later in this chapter.

> In mathematics, the Cartesian coordinate system specifies each point in two-dimensional space with a pair of numerical coordinates, which represents the distances from the nominal point at which the two axes meet. Cartesian coordinates may also be represented using complex numbers.
>
> In mathematics, the Polar coordinate system specifies a point in a two-dimensional space coordinate system, wherein each point on a plane is determined by a distance from a fixed point and an angle from a fixed direction.

Creating and manipulating spectra

Much unlike waveforms, which can only convey limited information on how a signal sounds, spectra, to some extent, reflect the way we perceive sound, and therefore the shape of a spectrum is a very straightforward indication of how a signal will sound. This explains why spectral synthesis techniques are very common. Here we will assume that the reader is already accustomed with basic techniques, such as additive or subtractive synthesis and amplitude/frequency modulation, and rather emphasize less obvious ways to synthesize or manipulate spectra.

Aggregating and enriching spectra

The most straightforward way to synthesize a custom spectrum would be to simply aggregate individual signals of a known spectral content together. The idea is obviously following the well-known additive synthesis paradigm, yet we extend this stratagem here to any kind of signal and not merely sinusoids. In such a context, we can use pure sine waves to pointillistically add specific frequencies, more complex oscillators to create series of harmonically related partials, and band-limited (that is, filtered) aperiodic generators to add energy in consecutive frequency ranges. Moreover, we can use control signals to dynamically control how our spectra will evolve in the course of time. We can easily extend this technique to the frequency-domain using `PV_Add`, which simply performs spectral addition. In the following code, we use a series of individually modulated units to synthesize a time-varying periodical spectrum:

```
( // synthesizing spectra by aggregating time-domain signals
Server.default.waitForBoot({ // boot server
    {    // amplitude-varying sine wave
        SinOsc.ar(540,mul:SinOsc.kr(0.1,pi).range(0,0.3))
        // amplitude-varying band-limited noise wave
        + Resonz.ar(ClipNoise.ar,3000,0.1,mul:SinOsc.kr(0.05).
          range(0,1))
        // frequency-varying sawtooth oscillator
        + Saw.ar(LFTri.kr(0.1).range(200,260),mul:0.2)
        // amplitude-varying additive synthesis (3 partials)
        + ( Klang.ar('[[800, 803, 811],[0.3, 0.7, 0.4],
          [0, 0, pi]]) *
        SinOsc.kr(0.5).range(0,1) );
    }.scopeResponse;
});
)
```

We can see the spectrum in the following screenshot:

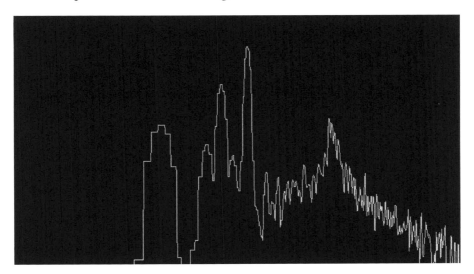

Sometimes we may want to enrich, that is add harmonics to, an existing spectrum so that everything we add follows the original spectrum's permutations over time. However, adding harmonics is neither possible nor meaningful for all kinds of signals. Our best chances are with simple oscillators or spectra consisting of a few partials only. We can easily add harmonics to such spectra relying either on the good old amplitude/frequency/ring modulation, which we will assume is already known here, or with standard waveshaping. For example:

```
//adding harmonics with clip
{Mix.new(SinOsc.ar((1..5)*LFNoise2.ar(10).range(200,500)))}.
scopeResponse; // original
{LeakDC.ar((Mix.new(SinOsc.ar((1..5)*LFNoise2.ar(10)
.range(200,500))).clip))}.scopeResponse; // with harmonics added
```

Remember that whenever using waveshaping techniques, as already discussed in the previous chapter, we should always have to be careful for potential time-domain side effects, such as DC-bias. While we can suspect DC problems by the presence of excessive energy in the lowest bins, it is a good idea to use a standard Stethoscope when experimenting with spectral synthesis.

Sculpting and freezing spectra

The polar opposite to aggregating spectra would be removing or manipulating specific partials of a complex one, much like a sculptor. In the time domain, we can easily do this by using standard filters or resonators. For example:

```
( // sculpting a spectrum in the time-domain
{ var signal = ClipNoise.ar(0.1); // start with a signal
rich in partials
    signal =
      DynKlank.ar('[[400,800,1300,4000],nil,[0.3,1,0.4,1]],signal,
      SinOsc.kr(0.1).range(0.5,4)); // use a bank of resonators to
      sculpt away partials and modulate their resonant frequencies
    signal = BPF.ar(signal, 2000,0.1); // band-pass filter
to remove more from the original
}.scopeResponse;
)
```

The subsequent screenshot demonstrates the spectrum:

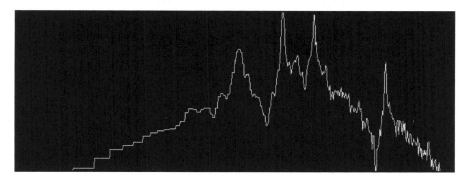

We have more options in the frequency domain; however, we could use `PV_BrickWall` (or its interpolated flavor `PV_Cutoff`) as very drastic low-pass filters, `PV_MagAbove` or `PV_MagBelow` to clear off selected bins above or below some threshold, `PV_MagClip` to clip partials to a certain threshold, `PV_MagSmear` to average magnitudes with respect to adjacent amplitudes, or `PV_RectComb` to create periodic magnitude gaps (much alike in a comb). For instance:

```
( // sculpt a complex spectra with PV_ Ugens
{var sound = FFT(LocalBuf(512),ClipNoise.ar()); // start with a
complex spectrum
sound = PV_BrickWall(sound,SinOsc.kr(0.5).range(0,0.1)); //filter off
the low end
    sound =PV_RectComb(sound,SinOsc.kr(0.2).range(2,7),0,
SinOsc.kr(1).range(0,0.5)); // create a varying number of gaps of
varying width
    sound = IFFT(sound);  // synthesize the time-domain signal
}.scopeResponse;
)
```

The following screenshot shows the spectrum:

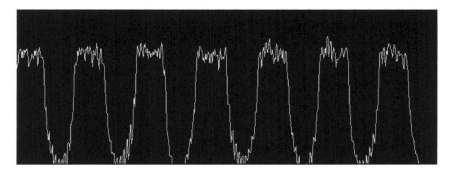

Another very common frequency-domain technique is that of momentarily freezing the spectra, an operation meaningful only for time-varying spectra, of course. We can freeze all bins or solely their magnitudes using PV_Freeze or PV_MagFreeze, respectively. The latter does not freeze changes in phase data and therefore, bins will have the same magnitude but spectral changes within each bin will pass through. In both cases, all we need to do is set the freeze argument to a non-zero value whenever we want our spectrum frozen. For instance:

```
( // freezing spectra
var buffer = Buffer.read(Server.default, Platform.resourceDir +/+
  "sounds/a11wlk01.wav"); // read a soundfile into the buffer
{var signal = PlayBuf.ar(1,buffer,BufRateScale.kr(buffer),loop:1);
    signal = FFT(LocalBuf(1024),signal);
    signal = PV_Freeze(signal,Duty.kr(1,0,Dseq([0,1],inf))); //
freeze signal every other second
    signal = IFFT(signal); // synthesize time-domain equivalent
}.scopeResponse;
)
```

Shifting, stretching, and scrambling spectra

Another common frequency-domain technique is to displace the position of the partials in a spectrum. We can easily shift or stretch them using the PV_BinShift or the PV_MagShift (the latter will affect the position of only the magnitudes of each bin). Their use is straightforward; we just provide a *stretch* factor to scale bins (or magnitudes) accordingly and a *shift* offset to move the whole spectrum to the left or the right. In the following example we periodically stretch and shift the magnitudes of a given spectrum:

```
( // shifting and stretching magnitudes
var buffer = Buffer.read(server.default, Platform.resourceDir +/+
  "sounds/a11wlk01.wav"); // read a soundfile into the buffer
{   var signal =
      PlayBuf.ar(1,buffer,BufRateScale.kr(buffer),loop:1);
// playback the soundfile
    signal = FFT(LocalBuf(1024),signal); // spectral analysis
    signal = PV_MagShift(signal,
        stretch: LFTri.kr(0.1).range(0.2,4), // stretch magnitudes
        shift: LFTri.kr(0.07).range(0,100) // shift magnitudes
    );
    signal = IFFT(signal) * 0.5; // synthesize time-domain equivalent
}.scopeResponse;
)
```

Another way to displace partials is to randomly scramble them using the PV_BinScramble UGen. We can define how many bins should be scrambled (setting the *wipe* argument from zero (for none) to one (for all)) and their maximum allowed deviation (setting the *width* again from zero to one). We can also force it to generate new random orderings by means of sending an audio trigger. In the following example, scramble all bins and then gradually morph back to the original spectrum:

```
(// scrambling bins
var buffer = Buffer.read(Server.default, Platform.resourceDir +/+
  "sounds/a11wlk01.wav"); // read a soundfile into the buffer
{var signal = PlayBuf.ar(1,buffer,BufRateScale.kr(buffer),loop:1);
    signal = FFT(LocalBuf(1024),signal);
    signal = PV_BinScramble(signal,Line.kr(1,0,15),1);
// scramble bins
    signal = IFFT(signal) * 0.5; // synthesize time-domain equivalent
}.scopeResponse;
)
```

There are other UGens that we can use to randomize spectra too, such as PV_RandComb, which will create random gaps in our spectrum or PV_Diffuser, which will shift each bin with a random phase offset. For example:

```
(// random gaps and phase offsets
var buffer = Buffer.read(Server.default, Platform.resourceDir +/+
  "sounds/a11wlk01.wav"); // read a soundfile into the buffer
{var signal = PlayBuf.ar(1,buffer,BufRateScale.kr(buffer),loop:1);
    signal = FFT(LocalBuf(1024),signal);
    signal = PV_RandComb(signal, LFNoise0.kr(1).range(0.3,1));
// add random gaps, modulately randomly
    signal = PV_Diffuser(signal,Impulse.kr(1)); // randomly bias
phases, new distributions every second
    signal = IFFT(signal); // synthesize time-domain equivalent
}.scopeResponse;
)
```

Using the pvcalc method

We can manually modify a frequency-domain signal using the PV_ChainUGen's pvcalc method with our own custom function as argument. Our function must return an array containing two arrays: one with the desired magnitudes and one with the desired phases. The function will be passed an array with the input's magnitudes and an array with the input's phases as arguments. Subsequently, we can calculate the output either with respect to the input or independently. We can also pinpoint a specific range of bins by means of the *frombin* and *tobin* parameters. Note that in all cases, the returning arrays have to be of an adequate size, which is either half that of the FFT window plus one, or equal to the custom range set with *frombin/tobin*. In the following example, we explicitly create three spectra with energy in specific bins and alternate through them using demand-rate UGens:

```
( // using pvcalc to create a custom spectrum
{ var sound = FFT(LocalBuf(512),Silent.ar()); // we start with silence
since we will populate the signal manually
    sound = sound.pvcalc(512,
        {    var magnitudes,phases;
            magnitudes = Array.fill(257,{arg i; if (i.isPowerOfTwo)
{1} {0} }); // for each of the numbers from 0 to 256, either 1 (if the
number is a power of two) or zero
            phases = Array.fill(257,{1.0.rand}); // random phases
            [magnitudes,phases] });  // return the signal
    sound = IFFT(sound) * 5;  // synthesize the time-domain equivalent
}.scopeResponse;
)
```

In this example, we start with silence (since we will replace the entire signal anyway), and then we invoke pvcalc with the FFT window's size and our custom function as the only arguments. Inside the function, we use Dseq to create a sequence of arrays that describe the magnitudes; we use an array with random values as phases. Note that the size of each returning array is half the size of the FFT window plus one (as defined internally in the FFT algorithm). In this case, we explicitly create the whole signal ourselves; however, we can easily use the pvcalc method to process some input spectrum, as in the following example, where we silence out a specific region of a spectrum:

```
( // replace the 100th to 200th partials in a 512 window
{   var sound = FFT(LocalBuf(512),ClipNoise.ar());
// we start with clip noise
    sound = sound.pvcalc(512,{
        arg inMags, inPhases;  // input's magnitudes and phases are
passed as arguments
        var outMags, outPhases;
```

```
        outMags = 0 ! 101;   // fill an array with 101 zeroes
        outPhases = inPhases[100..200]; // copy the input's 100th to
200th partials' phases
        [outMags,outPhases]}, // return 101 magnitudes and 101 phases
        frombin:100,tobin:200);   // replace the 100th-200th partials
of the input with the ones we generated herein
    sound = IFFT(sound)*0.5; // synthesize time-domain signal
}.scopeResponse;
)
```

Visualizing spectra

Unlike waveform scoping, the spectral one is idiosyncratic. Deciphering or
fine-tuning the spectral visualizations can be subtler and more involved as to
be explained here.

Limitations of spectral scoping

When scoping the spectra, we get a time-varying representation of them as
fluctuations of energy per bin. The horizontal axis represents the continuum of the
frequency range (typically from DC to the **Nyquist frequency**), divided in discrete
frequency ranges (that is, the bins). The vertical axis stands for the magnitude of
energy of the bins. Accordingly, each point in the graph represents the energy
of a particular frequency range (and not that of singleton partials). The graph
is constantly updated with respect to the FFT temporal window; once the FFT
algorithm has analyzed the snapshot of our signal, the graph is updated to represent
it. As already explained, the more time-accurate a spectral scope is, the less number
of bins it can accurately represent.

As discussed in *Chapter 1, Scoping, Plotting, and Metering*, we can typically select
between linear (that is, all bins have the same width in the horizontal axis) or
logarithmic (that is, bins in the lower register occupy larger regions than those in
the higher one) scaling to achieve a representation closer to the way we perceive
sound. (Note, however, that scopeResponse will always result in logarithmically
scaled graphs). In either mode, the resolution of the spectral visualization does not
depend exclusively on the specifics of the FFT analysis but also on the dimensions of
the View we use. SuperCollider will not complain if we use a 400px-width View to
visualize 4096 bins; yet, since it is impossible to fit them all, we would end up with a
graph illustrating approximately 10 percent of the available spectral information. This
is a pretty serious limitation given that we are always restrained with the physical
dimensions of our screen. Evidently, the spectral analysis resolution should ideally
match the width of the scoping View, or we may end up with both low spectral
resolution and slower update rates than what the FFT algorithm may deliver.

Another serious limitation is that FFT is not a linear process. Even when visualizing a single sinusoid, the scope will erroneously indicate that the spectral energy exists to a broader area, as FFT analysis will typically create artificial ramps around any isolated partials. Such artifacts and inaccuracies are not related with the scope per se, but on intrinsic limitations related with the underlying mathematical formulas and the very nature of discrete signals.

 The Nyquist frequency, named after electronic engineer *Harry Nyquist*, is the half of the sampling rate of the signal processing system and represents the highest frequency that this system can accurately reproduce.

Optimizing spectra for scoping

To some extent and depending on the context, we can compensate for some of the limitations mentioned earlier. The first step would be to decide whether a linear or a logarithmic representation is better for our particular application. We can then pinpoint the amplitude range that interests us setting dbRange accordingly (in an instance of FreqScopeView). Unfortunately, in its current implementation, FreqScopeView does not allow us to set a custom frequency region. Therefore, if we want to pinpoint specific bins, we need to come up with a hack: we can have FreqScopeView with extraordinary large bounds, and position it inside a smaller Window (or CompositeView) object so that only the part we are interested in is visible (the rest will be out of bounds). In the next example, just by means of tweaking the amplitude range and via this ingenious hack, we will visualize the first example of this chapter in a very different way:

```
( // pinpoint on a certain frequency range only
// the window
var window =  Window("Optimized FreqScoping", Rect(0, 0, 600,
  300)).front.onClose_({ freqScope.kill; sound.free; });
// the freqscope
// the signal
var sound = {SinOsc.ar(540,mul:SinOsc.kr(0.1,pi).range(0,0.3))
    + Resonz.ar(ClipNoise.ar,3000,0.1,mul:SinOsc.kr(0.05).
      range(0,1))
    + Saw.ar(LFTri.kr(0.1).range(200,260),mul:0.2)
    + ( Klang.ar('[[800, 803, 811],[0.3, 0.7, 0.4],[0, 0, pi]]) *
        SinOsc.kr(0.5).range(0,1) );
}.play;
var freqScope = FreqScopeView(window, Rect(-600,0,2100,300))
// notice the dimensions
```

```
.active_(true).freqMode_(1); // logarithmic scaling
freqScope.background_(Color.cyan);
freqScope.waveColors_([Color.red]);
freqScope.dbRange_(30); // custom db range
)
```

We could even use a scrolling Window object (just set `scroll` to `true`) if we want to achieve better resolution, and still be able to focus on various parts of the spectrum. Much like what we did in the previous chapter, we could also use instances of `Bus`, and various synthesis techniques to optimize our signals for frequency scoping. For example, we could use `PV_MagAbove` to focus only on the most prominent partials, or we could stretch our spectrum using `PV_BinShift` so that some particular range of bins we are interested in expands to a greater area and is better appreciated. Traditional time-domain filters, such as BPF, LPF, HPF, and BRF, could be very helpful in allowing us to smoothly filter off the energy in bins that we are not interested in visualizing. Depending on the context, we could even try more adventurous optimizations, for instance, using `PV_Freeze` to freeze the partials at regular intervals. Consider yet another way to frequency-scope the previous signal:

```
( // optimizing spectrum for frequency-scoping
// Window
var window = Window("Optimized FreqScoping", Rect(0, 0, 600,
    300)).front.onClose_({ freqScope.kill; sound.free; });
// audio bus
var bus = Bus.audio(Server.default);
// sound
var sound = {    var signal;
    signal = SinOsc.ar(540,mul:SinOsc.kr(0.1,pi).range(0,0.3))
    + Resonz.ar(ClipNoise.ar,3000,0.1,mul:SinOsc.kr(0.05).range(0,1))
    + Saw.ar(LFTri.kr(0.1).range(200,260),mul:0.2)
    + ( Klang.ar('[[800, 803, 811],[0.3, 0.7, 0.4],[0, 0, pi]]) *
        SinOsc.kr(0.5).range(0,1) );
    Out.ar(0,signal); // write to audio output
    // optimize for scoping
    signal = FFT(LocalBuf(4096),signal);
    signal = PV_BinShift(signal,4);
// stretch bins for better resolution
    signal = PV_MagAbove(signal,3); // do not show weak bins
    signal = IFFT(signal);
    Out.ar(bus,signal); // write to bus
}.play;
var freqScope = FreqScopeView(window,
    Rect(0,0,600,300)).active_(true).freqMode_(0).inBus_(bus);
// set freq-scope to read from bus
freqScope.background_(Color.cyan);
freqScope.waveColors_([Color.red]);
freqScope.dbRange_(80); // custom db range
)
```

In the following figure, we can see how the last two visualizations compare with the original:

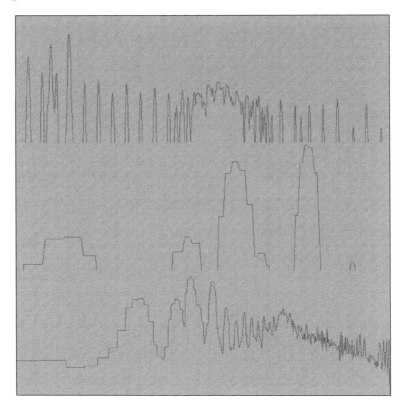

Summary

In this chapter, we discussed a series of audio synthesis techniques to synthesize new, or manipulate pre-existent, spectra so that we are capable of creating optimized, ready-to-scope signals in the frequency domain too.

In the next chapter, we will introduce the fundamentals of computer graphics and learn how to draw shapes and structures of arbitrary complexity in SuperCollider using the Pen class.

4
Vector Graphics

So far, we have elaborated on how to scope, plot, and meter signals and data as well as on how to create good-looking, (in any subjective way) ready-to-scope audio signals. In this chapter, we will introduce ourselves with two-dimensional vector graphics, and we will learn how to use the `Pen` class to generate shapes of arbitrary complexity as well as more sophisticated structures such as fractals and particle systems. It has to be said that while SuperCollider is arguably less featured than other dedicated computer graphics environments, such as the various OpenGL-based frameworks, it is nevertheless powerful enough and a lot easier to master; more importantly, it is also bundled with one of the most advanced audio synthesis engines on the planet, thereby, simplifying the task of integrating **Computer-generated Imagery (CGI)** with computer-generated audio.

The topics that will be covered in this chapter are as follows:

- Learning the vector graphics fundamentals
- Drawing simple and complex shapes
- Modeling complex objects and structures
- Geometrical transformations and trailing effects
- Designing particle systems and fractals

Learning the vector graphics fundamentals

Generating vector graphics involves formally describing a drawing in mathematical terms by means of geometrical primitives, graphics state transformations, and simple drawing instructions. In this context, a drawing consists of *paths*, which are made of one or more line segments connected by two or more *anchor points*. Paths are to be delimited in our *canvas* (that is, the `View` we draw into) using Cartesian coordinates, which are pairs in the form of (x,y) where x and y denote the horizontal and vertical deviations respectively from a nominal point. We may speak of absolute coordinates when the nominal (0,0) point is fixed in space; relative coordinates are those that are relative to some other arbitrary points. An (x,y) pair can be also understood as a complex number with x representing the real and y the imaginary part, thus simplifying mathematical operations in certain contexts. To represent coordinates in SuperCollider, we use instances of `Point`, which can be also created using the convenient form: `x@y`. Unlike the traditional Cartesian notation, the `0@0` point in SuperCollider stands for the upper-left corner of some `View`, with x incrementing rightward and y downward. Once we have defined the anchor points of a path, we can sketch it by means of combining straight lines and curves or built-in primitive shapes, defining colors, thicknesses of various lines, and various other graphics state attributes.

Vector graphics need to be rendered to pixels before they are sent to our screen, which requires a conversion to **raster graphics**, yet this approach has significant advantages over drawing raster graphics in the first place. For instance, when zooming in to some detail in the vector domain, we preserve the maximum resolution since we merely render a different set of instructions rather than magnifying individual pixels. More importantly, we can easily prototype complex structures and transformations as minimal sets of instructions so that we can later generate contingent instances of these efficiently and in different contexts. But even if it wasn't for efficiency reasons, there are other reasons that affect their performance; it is a lot faster to perform mathematical operations on a limited number of anchor points, rather than scanning and altering the state of multidimensional matrices of pixels.

Paths are shapes or line segments delimited and used as the building blocks of all drawings in a vector graphics context.

Anchor points are those points that delimit a path in a vector graphics context.

Raster graphics is an alternative to the vector graphics paradigm, wherein, a drawing is represented as a dot matrix structure with the color values of each of the individual pixels necessary to print or project it to some medium.

Pixels are either the elementary atoms of some raster image or the smallest, addressable element in a display device such as a computer screen.

Drawing primitive shapes and loading images

In SuperCollider, we can draw simple lines and basic shapes invoking the appropriate methods from Pen inside the drawfunc method of Window. There are primitives for arcs, lines, rectangles, ellipses, and wedges. For example:

```
( // primitive shapes with Pen
var window = Window("Pen Example", 450@450).front; // a window
window.drawFunc_({  // all the drawing has to be done in this function
  Pen.line(0@0,100@100);              // a line between 2 points
  Pen.line(350@100,450@0);            // a line between 2 points
  Pen.addArc(200@150,20,0,pi);        // half a circle (an arc with
angle of pi radians)
  Pen.addArc(250@200,40,pi,pi/2);     // 1/4th of a circle
  Pen.addRect(Rect(50,100,350,300));  // a rectangle
  Pen.addOval(Rect(100,220,250,80));  // an ellipse
  Pen.addWedge(350@350,40,1.5pi,pi/2); // a pi/2 radians wedge
  Pen.addAnnularWedge(345@355,15,40,0,1.5pi); // and an annular wedge
  Pen.stroke;   // draw only the outlines
});
)
```

In this example, no drawing will occur unless we explicitly instruct `Pen` to do so and after having defined the desired paths, we used `*stroke` to only draw their outlines. Every path has a *stroke* (that is, an outline) and a *fill* (that is, the surface delimited by its outline) area that we can selectively draw using `*stroke` (stroke only), `*fill` (fill only), or `*fillStroke` (both strokes and fills). There also exists a `*draw` method, which will draw paths according to the given argument. The numbers 0, 2, and 3 are equivalent to `fill`, `stroke`, and `fillStroke` respectively and 1 and 4 are for drawing either fills or stroke and fills, following the even-odd rule. This rule guarantees that the adjacent areas will not be filled so that the internal fragmentation of some path is always respected. We can also load and display images in our canvas using the `Image` class. However, note that `Image` is not functional in the current (as of this writing) SuperCollider stable Version (3.6). We need to use 3.7, which is already available as a source code bundle, to evaluate the following code:

```
( // loading and displaying images
var image = Image.new("path/to/some/png/image/here");
// load some image
Window.new.front.drawFunc_({
    image.drawAtPoint(0@0,image.bounds); // display image
})
)
```

Of course, instead of the dummy `path/to/some/png/image/here`, we are expected to provide a valid path pointing to a real file in our computer. To only display a part of an image, we could have passed an instance of `Rect` instead of their bounds.

Complex shapes and graphics state

We can easily draw custom shapes of arbitrary complexity by means of simply connecting anchor points together with line segments using the methods: `*moveTo`, `*arcTo`, `*lineTo`, `*curveTo`, and `*quadCurveTo` (quadratic curves). The `*moveTo` method merely sets the current position of `Pen` to some point, while the rest of the methods create segments, whatever the current position may be, to some ending point that was already provided; this will be subsequently casted to the new position. These directives stand for arcs, lines, and **Bezier curves**. For example:

```
( // generating a custom path
var window = Window("Pen Example", 450@450).front;
window.drawFunc_({
  Pen.moveTo(78@122);                    // go to point 70@122
  Pen.curveTo(284@395,280@57,78@122);
/* make a Bezier curve from 78@122 to 284@395 (which is now the new
current position). 280@57 and 78@122 are curvature points */
  Pen.curveTo(280@57,80@332,284@395); // make another Bezier curve
  Pen.curveTo(80@332,405@225,280@57); // make another Bezier curve
  Pen.curveTo(405@225,78@122,80@332); // make another Bezier curve
```

```
    Pen.curveTo(78@122,284@395,405@225); // make another Bezier curve
    Pen.draw(4);  // fill according to the even-odd rule
  });
  )
```

One important thing to note is that if we had invoked *draw prior to having all of the segments described, we would have ended up with a very different drawing. Only those segments between the drawing methods are assigned to the same path. The reader is invited to try and insert more Pen.draw(4) statements between the Bezier curves in the preceding code and find out for himself/herself. Pen also features a set of methods and variables to change the graphics state itself, for example, *width (changes the width of the stroke), *smoothing (switches anti-aliasing on/off for smoother images), *joinStyle (changes the way lines are joined), *lineDash (sets up a dash line pattern), *alpha (sets global transparency), and others to be discussed in detail shortly. Note that graphics state transformations are always cumulative and will affect all of the subsequent drawing commands unless they are reset.

 Bézier curves are parametric curves named after the French engineer *Pierre Bézier* who first systemized their study in the '60s.

Introducing colors, transparency, and gradients

Adding color to our drawing is easy using the *fillColor or *strokeColor variables of Pen to define colors for the fill and the stroke of our paths, and the background variable of window to set the background color of the canvas. As with all **graphics state transformations**, once we set a specific color, it will be casted with the new default value until we explicitly set another. Colors in SuperCollider are represented as instances of the Color class. Typical use is either through convenient methods (such as *red, *white, *black, *yellow, and so on) or by means of describing the color in terms of its *RGBA* (*Red, Green, Blue,* and *Alpha*) or its *HSVA* (*Hue, Saturation, Value,* and *Alpha*) coefficients, where saturation signifies colorfulness and value signifies brightness. The **Alpha channel** stands for how transparent or opaque a color is. We can create specific colors via *new (expects Float in the range of 0 to 1), *new255 (expects Integer in the range of 0 to 255), *fromHexString (expects an eight-character-long string with the RGBA coefficients in hexadecimal notation, that is, in the range of 00-FF), or *hsv (expects the HSVA coefficients as Float) methods. Other useful methods to remember are *rand, which will generate a random color, and the various binary operators such as add, subtract, multiply, divide, and blend among others. Consider the following example:

```
( // transparency and custom color example
var window = Window("Pen Example", 450@450).front;
window.background_(Color.white); // set background color
window.drawFunc_({
  Pen.width_(10);       // set stroke width as 10 pixels
  Pen.strokeColor_(Color.cyan);  // set cyan as stroke color
  Pen.fillColor_(Color.fromHexString("FF0000FF"));
// set red as fill color
  Pen.addRect(Rect(30,30,300,300)); // add a rectangle
  Pen.draw(4);   // draw rectangle
  Pen.strokeColor_(Color.rand);  // set a random color as stroke
  Pen.fillColor_(Color.new255(0,255,0,50));
// set a transparent green as fill color
  Pen.addRect(Rect(220,220,200,200)); // draw another rectangle
  Pen.draw(4);   // draw
});
)
```

Apart from solid colors, we can also fill our paths using **gradients**, that is, smooth progressions between two colors. Gradients come in two flavors: *axial gradients*, specified by two points and a color at each point, and *radial gradients*, specified by one color at the outer perimeter of a circular arc and another at its center. In both cases, the colors in the middle are calculated with linear interpolation. The Pen class has two corresponding methods: *fillAxialGradient and *fillRadialGradient. For example:

```
( // custom path with gradient
var window = Window("Pen Example", 450@450).front.drawFunc_({
  Pen.moveTo(78@122);
  Pen.curveTo(284@395,280@57,78@122);
  Pen.curveTo(280@57,80@332,284@395);
  Pen.curveTo(80@332,405@225,280@57);
  Pen.curveTo(405@225,78@122,80@332);
  Pen.curveTo(78@122,284@395,405@225);
     Pen.fillRadialGradient(225@225, 225@225, 0,250,Color.red, Color.
green);
});
)
```

As we can see in the following screenshot, the preceding code results in a windmill-like shape:

Abstractions and models

Suppose that we really like the particular shape in the preceding screenshot and that we want to integrate it in a series of different drawings, in other words, to cast it as a **sprite** (that is, an independent structure integrated to a broader scheme). Of course, having to manually define the positions of the anchor points for each different case would be tedious, counterintuitive, and really shortsighted from a programmer's point of view, so we need to come up with some kind of abstraction. We could just put all the necessary instructions inside a function and make all the calculations relative to its arguments. However, this approach proves shortsighted too, as sooner or later we will encounter situations wherein we would want to interact with our shape after it's being created. What we really need is an abstract prototype we could use to spawn unique independent instances of our structure that we can later interact with. Furthermore, using prototypes, we can easily go beyond modeling simple sprites to modeling whole families of contingent structures, such as windmills having different number of wings, different color combinations, and different positioning and sizes.

Objects and prototypes

SuperCollider being a purely object-oriented programming language fosters object modeling through `Class`, `Environment`, or `Event`—every approach having its pros and cons. Using classes in SuperCollider is a bit idiosyncratic; we have to recompile the whole class library every time we make some minor change to a definition, and more to this, it's not really intuitive to have all sorts of project-specific classes globally available every time we launch SuperCollider. Classes are ideal when we want to extend SuperCollider's overall functionality with objects we will either plan to use very often or with features we want to be globally available, such as the custom scope meter we designed in *Chapter 1, Scoping, Plotting, and Metering*. As far as projects of more limited scope are concerned, such as our windmill herein, using `Event` makes more sense. Also, it's always easier to convert the latter into a `Class`, if we do happen to use it that often, rather than the opposite.

Notwithstanding, there are certain caveats to using `Event` as an object prototype. Firstly, we should never use names for our variables or methods that match the existent `Event` (or its superclasses'), for instance, `size`, `at`, `play`, `resume`, `pause`, `release`, `update`, `fill`, `use`, `test`, and others. Doing so will certainly lead to very obscure and difficult-to-track bugs. A fast way to get a complete reference of all problematic names is to type `Event` and press *command + I* (or *Ctrl + I*) while in the SCide. Secondly, we should be extremely cautious about typos, as the interpreter will not complain if we attempt to access or set some nonexistent entry. Thirdly, SuperCollider does not support private membership (this is also true for classes unfortunately), therefore, we cannot easily distinguish between a model's *interface* (that is, methods and data the user is supposed to access) and its *implementation* (that is, methods and data for internal use that should be hidden from the user).

We will soon describe how to partly compensate for this; it is a good tactic, nevertheless, to only interact with objects following certain conventions. Throughout this book, we will only interact with our objects via methods such as `refresh`, `animate`, or `draw` and will never directly set some member variable. For instance, the structure of a windmill object could appear as shown in the following code:

```
( // Event as an object prototype
    position: /* sprite's position */,
    points: /* the anchor points */,
    refresh: { arg self, newPosition;
        // set new position and recalculate anchor points here
    },
    draw: { arg self;
        // draw path here
    }
)
```

Notice that the first argument in every method is always named `self`. This is a standard mechanism to share data inside our object; every method will be implicitly passed the whole `Event` as an argument so that we can easily access other member variables and methods from within. This argument is not visible externally when invoking `refresh`, in this case, only one argument, `newPosition`, will be considered.

Factories

Having modeled a windmill object, we also need a mechanism to create and initialize instances of it, namely, a windmill **factory**. The idea is to use an instance of `Function` with the desired attributes of our windmills as arguments and have it define, initialize, and return an instance of it. A significant gain in this approach is that now we can define private data members and methods within the body of our function that will only be accessible to our object's methods and not to its clients, thereby, achieving information hiding, which is a key concept in more sophisticated object-oriented designs yet not directly supported by some built-in structure. Another important plus is that we can now segregate between defining, initializing, and using an object so that we only perform those calculations when needed. Back to our example, a proper windmill factory should be capable of producing more than just one type of windmill, all having different number of wings, size, and colors. Carefully considering what the interface of our factory should be is the first step towards designing it. A possible structure for our windmill factory could look as shown in the following code:

```
{  arg position, radius, numOfWings, colors;
  var object;
    // ..private data/methods and auxiliary calculations here
    object = ( // define and initialize
      position: /* define and initialize position */,
      points: /* define and initialize anchor points */,
      refresh: { arg self, newPosition; // define refresh method
         // set newPosition here
        },
      draw: { arg self;  // define draw method
         // draw path here
        }
    );
    object; // explicitly return the object
};
```

And now all we have to do is programmatically describe the specifics of our object's construction and use, which of course, is a task largely dependent on the kind of object we are dealing with. In the windmill's case, we first need to calculate the angular distance between the wings so that we can space them accordingly, and then, via an iterative structure to calculate the starting, ending, and curvature points for each segment with respect to its position and radius. A possible windmill factory implementation is given in the following code. However, note that due to the nature of the math involved, and in order to keep things fairly simple, this particular factory will properly create windmills whose number of wings is not a multiple of 4 plus 6 (that is, $6+[n*4]$). Note also that only those operations needed for the actual drawing and updating exist within our body of Event. Everything related to initialization is calculated inside the factory's body and then either stored as a data member of our object (if it should ever be modulated, for instance, position or points) or hard coded into its methods' definitions (if it should be immutable, for example, numOfWings).

```
( // windmill factory
~windmillFactory = { arg position = 0@0, radius = 100,
    numberOfWings = 5, colors = [Color.red, Color.green];

  // calculate step (angular difference between consecutive points)
  var step = if (numberOfWings.odd) {
    (2pi / numberOfWings) * (numberOfWings/2).floor;
  } {
    (2pi / numberOfWings) * ((numberOfWings/2)-1);
  };

  // calculate points' coordinates and store in an array
  var points = Array.fill(numberOfWings, {
/* we only need one point per wing as they are connected with each
other diametrically */
    arg i;
    var x, y;
    x = position.x + (radius * cos((step * i)));
    y = position.y + (radius * sin((step * i)));
    x@y; // return the anchor point point
  });

  var windmill = ( // event as an object prototype
    position: position,  // sprite's position
    points: points,  // the anchor points (to be updated if needed)
    refresh: { arg self, newPosition;
      self.position = newPosition;  // set new position
      // re-calculate points according to newPosition
      self.points = Array.fill(numberOfWings, {
        arg i;
```

```
        var x, y;
        x = newPosition.x + (radius * cos((step * i)));
        y = newPosition.y + (radius * sin((step * i)));
        x@y; // return the anchor point point
      });
    },
    draw: { arg self;
      Pen.moveTo(self.points[0]); // move to the first point
      (numberOfWings).do{  // iterate over the array of anchor points
        arg i;
        var pointA, pointB, pointC;
        // get three consecutive points
        pointA = self.points[i];
        pointB = self.points.wrapAt(i+1);
        pointC = self.points.wrapAt(i+2);
        Pen.curveTo(pointB,pointC,pointA); // define Bezier segment
      };

      // fill with radial gradient
      Pen.fillRadialGradient(self.position, self.position,0,
        radius*1.5,colors[0], colors[1]);
    }
  );
  windmill;  // return windmill
};
)
```

We should save the preceding file independently so that we can automatically call it from our code and use it as follows:

```
( // draw windmills
var windmillA, windmillB, windmillC, windmillD;
(PathName(thisProcess.nowExecutingPath).pathOnly ++
"9677OS_04_06.scd").loadPaths; // first load the windmill factory
windmillA=~windmillFactory.(150@150,150,15,
[Color.red,Color.magenta]);
windmillB=~windmillFactory.(100@500,80,23);
windmillC=~windmillFactory.(500@100,100,5,
[Color.magenta,Color.black]);
windmillD=~windmillFactory.(400@420,200,9,[Color.black,Color.blue]);
Window.new("Windmills",640@640).background_(Color.white).front.
drawFunc_({
  windmillA.draw();
  windmillB.draw();
  windmillC.draw();
  windmillD.draw();
});
)
```

Note that the proper way to load files is using `Document.current.dir`, which will return the path of the folder that contains the current file. Unfortunately this is broken in the current (as of this writing) version of SCide (however, it is functional in other IDEs such as emacs), therefore, we will have to either use the not so preferred `PathName(thisProcess.nowExecutingPath).pathOnly` or wait for the next major update.

> **Information hiding** is, in Computer Science, the principle of segregation between an object's interface (what the users of the object will encounter and use) and its implementation (intrinsic design details of which might change).
>
> **Object-oriented design** is a certain approach to software development wherein systems of interacting objects are used to solve a problem.

Geometrical transformations, matrices, and trailing effects

Geometrical transformations are operations that will map each individual point in a set to another unique point. They invaluably simplify the task of modeling some particular structure. The most important geometrical transformations are `*translate` (move the whole coordinate system by *x* and *y* offsets), `*scale` (scale a drawing according to scaling factors for the horizontal and vertical dimensions), `*skew` (skew paths with respect to the given coordinates), and `*rotate` (rotate the path around a given point). As is the case with all graphics state operations, geometrical transformations will affect all of the subsequent drawing commands and are cumulative. However, quite often, we will want to apply some geometrical or other transformations to a specific structure only, and some other times, we will need to revert to an unknown graphics state (for example, when transformation occurs within the `draw` method of some prototype, we want them to be valid only locally and revert to the previous state, whatever it may be).

Luckily, there are simple ways to deal with such situations, namely, using the *transformation matrices*, which are really nothing more than just a description of the current graphic's state. Whenever we want to apply geometrical transformations or otherwise alter the graphic's state (for example, setting a different color) in a given context only, we can simply *push* a new matrix wherein we will apply all our transformations; once done, we can *pop* (destroy) it to revert to the previous graphic's state. Push and pop are operations associated with *stack*, which is a Last-In-First-Out (LIFO) container, which is used internally to hold an arbitrary number of matrices. In this way, we can easily revert to a default graphics state and in addition to this, we can efficiently stack an arbitrary number of matrices on top of each other. A standard way to handle matrices in SuperCollider is via the *use method of Pen, which will evaluate an instance of Function within a new matrix and then revert to the previous graphic's state automatically. Therefore, and since Pen does cater for a *push and a *pop method, we will stick with those methods throughout this book for reasons of conceptual clarity as well as because this is the standard way most major computer graphics frameworks handle matrices anyway. In the following code, we perform basic geometrical transformations to create trailing effects with our windmills:

```
( // trailing effects using geometrical transformations
(PathName(thisProcess.nowExecutingPath).pathOnly ++
"9677OS_04_06.scd").loadPaths; // first load the windmill factory

Window("Trailing Effects Example",640@480).background_(Color.white).
front.drawFunc_({
  // trailing effects with rotation
  Pen.push;  // push a new matrix
  5.do{ arg i;
    var windmill = ~windmillFactory.value(150@200,130,11);
// create 5 instances of an 11-winged windmill
    Pen.rotate(i * 0.1,150,200);
// incrementally rotate each instance around its own axis
    Pen.alpha_(1-(i*0.1));  // decrementally set transparency
    windmill.draw();        // draw the windmills
  };
  Pen.pop; // pop matrix to revert to original graphics state

  // trailing effects with translation
  Pen.push;  // push a new matrix
  10.do{ arg i;
```

```
      var windmill = ~windmillFactory.(420@120,130,7);
// create 10 instances of a 7-winged windmill
      Pen.translate(10,10);
/* cummulatively translate each instance 10 pixels upwards and
downwards */
      Pen.alpha_(1-(i*0.1)); // decrementally set transparency
      windmill.draw();  // draw the windmills
    };
  Pen.pop;  // pop matrix to revert to original graphics state

  // trailing effects with scaling
  Pen.push;       // push a new matrix
  3.do{ arg i;
      var windmill = ~windmillFactory.(80@400,60,7);
// create 3 instances of a 7-winged windmill
      Pen.scale(1.7,1);
// cummulatively scale each instance's horizontal dimension
      Pen.alpha_(1-(i*0.1)); // decrementally set transparency
      windmill.draw(); // draw the windmills
    };
  Pen.pop;  // pop matrix to revert to original graphics state
});
)
```

The following screenshot illustrates the result:

Complex structures

We can achieve more sophisticated structures and systems of arbitrary complexity by means of combining individual sprites, transformations, and a set of specialized techniques. Typical examples are the particle systems or the fractals.

Particle systems

A **particle system** is the granular synthesis (that is to synthesize complex sounds by means of using elementary sonic grains) equivalent to a computer graphics context, wherein we generate complex visual structures by means of dispersing elementary particles in space. The latter are usually, but not exclusively, instances of the same prototype. Much like a granular synthesis engine, we typically permute each particle's appearance to allow divergence. Particles may be distributed in space in a number of ways according to canonical, noncanonical, and even more complex patterns. The following code randomly spreads windmills on our canvas:

```
( // An a-canonical particle system
var window = Window("An a-canonical particle system",640@480).
background_(Color.black).front;
(PathName(thisProcess.nowExecutingPath).pathOnly ++
"9677OS_04_06.scd").loadPaths; // first load the windmill factory
window.drawFunc_({ 500.do{       // iterate 500 times
    var x,y, radius, windmill;
    x = window.bounds.width.rand;  // a random x (but within bounds)
    y = window.bounds.height.rand; // a random y (but within bounds)
    radius = rrand(10,50);         // a random radius
    Pen.push;                      // push a new matrix
    Pen.alpha_(1.0.rand);     // set a random level of transparency
    Pen.rotate(2pi.rand,x,y);
// randomly rotate each particle around its own axis
    windmill = ~windmillFactory.value(x@y,radius,(5,7..25).choose,
[Color.rand,Color.rand]);
/* generate a windmill object centered at x@y with a random ratio, a
random even number of wings, and random colorings */
    windmill.draw(); // draw windmills
    Pen.pop;   // destroy matrix and revert to default state
}});
)
```

A possible result is shown in the following screenshot:

Note that when resizing our `Window`, its `drawFunc` will be evaluated again, so we will get a different random distribution. The following code demonstrates a canonical distribution this time:

```
( // A canonical particle system
var window = Window("A canonical particle system",640@480).background_
(Color.yellow).front;
(PathName(thisProcess.nowExecutingPath).pathOnly ++
"9677OS_04_06.scd").loadPaths; // first load the windmill factory
window.drawFunc_({
  forBy(0,window.bounds.width-50,50,{
// iterate over width minus 50 (to leave a margin) by steps of 50
    arg ix;
    forBy(0,window.bounds.height-50,50,{
/* for each iteration over width, iterate over height minus 50 (to
leave a margin) by steps of 50 */
      arg iy;
```

```
    var x,y,windmill; // coordinates and our windmill
    x = 45 + ix;
/* incrementally (by 50) calculate x, add offset it by 45 so that the
first element is not right on the edge */
    y = 45 + iy;
/* incrementally (by 50) calculate y, add offset it by 45 so that the
first element is not right on the edge */
    Pen.push; // push new matrix
    Pen.rotate(2pi.rand,x,y);
// randomly rotate each windmill around its own axis
        /* generate windmills so that each row has more wings than the
previous and so that colors are a function of position */
    windmill = ~windmillFactory.(x@y,20,(5,7..27).wrapAt(ix/50),
        [Color(sin(ix/50).abs,sin(iy/50).abs,1),
        Color.black]);
        windmill.draw(); // draw windmill
    Pen.pop; // pop matrix
  });
 });
});
)
```

Fractals

Fractals are structures characterized by replication too, yet of a very different kind. Fractals are characterized by some prominent patterns ever present in all scales; hence, they are self-similar. Fractals are everywhere in the natural world, consider for example, some coastline; it looks self-similar however much we zoom in or zoom out to/from some part of it. We can generate fractals of arbitrary complexity *recursively* or *iteratively*. In computer science, we may speak of recursion whenever a part of the definition of some function is a call to itself. A physical world analogy would be that of holding a mirror against another. Consider the following code wherein we compute factorials recursively:

```
f = {arg n; if  (n>1)  {n * f.value(n-1)} {1} }; // a recursive
function
f.(5).postln; // factorial of 5
```

In all recursive functions, it is imperative to use some kind of mechanism to prevent infinite function calls, a state also referred to as infinite recursion or *infinite loop*, which would crash the interpreter at once. In the factorial example, we used an `if` statement to ensure that however big n is, the recursive calls will indeed cease at some point. We can also use the `thisFunction` keyword instead of the function's own name to emphasize that we are indeed within a recursive structure; however, we should always assign it to some local variable to clarify what function we are referring to, otherwise, we may encounter very obscure bugs whenever nested functions are involved. We will follow this approach herein for reasons of conceptual clarity.

To create fractals, we need to define some drawing pattern, which will repeat itself on an arbitrary number of levels. Each level would consist of several branches, each being the parent of child branches and so on until the last level is reached, which would only feature its own branches. In the following example, we start from a central point and create line segments (our branches) that canonically spread in all directions. To achieve canonicity, all angles between the adjacent branches must be identical, thus equal to $2\pi/numBranches$ radians. Each branch starting at its own center (the center of the parent segment) will spawn its own children branches until the last level is reached. In actual programming practice and to avoid infinite loops, we typically start with a variable set at the maximum level and decrement it in subsequent recursive calls until we reach 0 when recursion seizes. Again, we will use a factory so that we can create contingent structures with different characteristics with respect to a number of levels, number of branches, size (radius), and a changing factor (used to modulate the amount of change between subsequent levels).

```
( // a fractal factory
~fractalFactory = { arg numLevels, numBranches, position, radius,
changeFactor;

  var fractalFunc = thisFunction;
// assign thisFunction to a variable
    var points, children, fractal; // declare variables
  // calculate ending points for our segments
  points = Array.fill(numBranches, {arg i;
    var x, y;
    x = position.x + (radius * numLevels * cos(((2pi/numBranches) *
i)));
    y = position.y + (radius * numLevels * sin(((2pi/numBranches) *
i)));
    x@y;
  });

  // generate children
  if (numLevels > 0) { // if there are more levels to go
    var childrenPoints, childrenRadius;
    // calculate the children points for each for the branches
    childrenPoints = Array.fill(numBranches, {arg i;
      var x,y;
      x = (points[i].x + position.x) / 2;
      y = (points[i].y + position.y) / 2;
      x@y
    });

    // calculate the children radiuses
    childrenRadius = radius * changeFactor;

    /* for each level generate all branches and add them to fChildren
array */
    numBranches.do{ arg i;
      children = children.add(fractalFunc.(numLevels-1, numBranches,
childrenPoints[i], childrenRadius, changeFactor));
    };

  } { // if there are more levels to go set children to nil
    children = nil;
  };
```

```
   // create fractal object
   fractal = (
     children: children,
/* an array with the children (all of them fractal objects, too or nil
if in the last level) */
     branches: numBranches,    // how many branches
     draw: {arg self, colorFunc; // drawing function,
       // draw self
       self.branches.do{arg i;
                Pen.strokeColor_(colorFunc.());
// set a color for each branch
          Pen.line(position,points[i]); // create lines
                Pen.stroke; // stroke lines
       };
       // draw children
       if (self.children.notNil) { // if there are children
         // draw all of their branches
         self.children.do{arg item;
           item.draw(colorFunc);
         };
       };
     };
   );

   fractal; // explicitly return fractal
};
)
```

The preceding code can be used as follows:

```
( // a fractal example
var window, fractal; // declare variables
    (PathName(thisProcess.nowExecutingPath).pathOnly ++
"9677OS_04_12.scd").loadPaths; // first load the windmill factory
window = Window("a fractal !", 640@640).background_(Color.black).
front;
fractal = ~fractalFactory.(6, 4,window.bounds.center,60,0.6);
window.drawFunc_({
  fractal.draw({Color.rand});
});
)
```

The preceding code results in a fractal as shown in the following screenshot:

Modulating our factory's arguments we may achieve a whole family of very different, albeit related, fractals. We could try with these settings for example:

```
~fractalFactory.(6, 6,window.bounds.center,100,0.5);
```

And this way, obtaining the image displayed in the following screenshot:

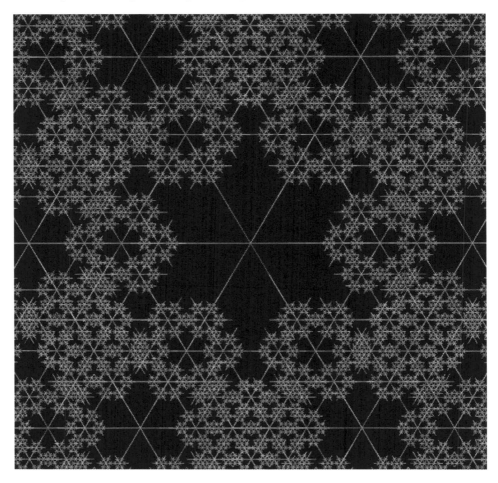

Fractals is a very intriguing, albeit mathematically involved subject. There are numerous kinds of fractals and numerous ways to implement them. The fractal factory herein is merely an example and should not be considered as a rule set in stone; nonetheless, it does exemplify how to handle the most fundamental concepts, namely, recursion levels and children branches. When dealing with fractals, we should always bear in mind that they are typical examples of the *exponential growth*. Consider that each additional level exponentially raises the recursive function calls since every single branch will automatically acquire additional levels, each of which will have several braches having several children each and so on. Fractals are greedy beings computationally, so we should always try with just a few levels/branches and gradually increment them to make sure of what our computer can handle.

Summary

Throughout this chapter, we introduced ourselves to both the fundamental and more advanced notions and techniques as far as two-dimensional vector graphics are concerned. Also, with numerous examples, we have demonstrated how to generate simple drawings as well as more sophisticated structures and shapes.

In the next chapter, we will discuss the types of motion and learn how to animate our singleton shapes as well as more complex structures in various ways.

5
Animation

In the previous chapter, we learned how to generate complex shapes and structures using Pen and a series of fundamental techniques. In this chapter, we will introduce ourselves to the fundamentals of motion, and we will learn how to animate vector graphics using UserView. A series of more advanced concepts and techniques are also discussed, such as how to simulate physical forces to make our animations behave in a more natural way and how to animate articulated bodies.

The topics that will be covered in this chapter are as follows:

- Fundamentals of motion
- Animating shapes and sprites
- Creating trailing effects
- User interaction and event-driven programming
- Animating particle systems and fractals
- Dynamics and kinematics

Fundamentals of motion

Animation is just a succession of different images that produces an illusion of movement. Therefore, to create interesting animations, we need to familiarize ourselves with the various ways in which we can set shapes, sprites, and more complex structures in motion, as well as with motion as a medium per se.

Motion species

Different kinds of motion evoke different emotional and cognitive responses. That is to say that motion has its own significance, which has to be carefully considered as a fundamental quality of a work, be it of artistic, scientific, or of any other nature. In a computer graphics context, we can distinguish between three basic types of motion:

- **Uniform motion**: In this type of motion, the direction and the speed of the moving object(s) are kept unchanged

- **Accelerated motion**: In this type of motion, the direction and the speed of the moving object(s) are dependent on various forces

- **Chaotic motion**: This type of motion is random and unpredictable to some degree

Uniform motion is almost absent in the physical world wherein gravity, friction, acceleration, and miscellaneous other forces affect the way objects move in a completely causal way. We could emulate this behavior within the context of accelerated motion, nevertheless, the latter may stand for motion dependent on any kind of forces, even uncanny, out-of-the-world ones; coherency and causality are not specific to reality. Chaotic motion is largely computer specific and is more or less dependent on complex stochastic equations to behave in an explicitly non-linear and unpredictable manner. We should be comfortable with all types of motions so that we can grant our animations a particular quality we are after in any given context. Of course, different kinds of motion can be integrated into the same scenery either temporarily or spatially so that we can achieve more complex scenarios.

Using UserView

Having discussed the different kinds of motion, we need mechanisms to implement them. The standard way to animate vector graphics in all major frameworks is through some sort of a **callback function**. This function will be typically evaluated several times per second (depending on the frame rate settings), each time calculating what the subsequent frame (that is, every individual image in the animating sequence) will look like. To animate something, we basically have to calculate how they should change for every consecutive frame and redraw them accordingly. Therefore, unlike traditional or stop-motion animation, computer animation is achieved simply by algorithmically describing how scenery will permute over time.

Animation in SuperCollider is primarily addressed through some specialized `UserView` class. This will evaluate its `drawFunc` several times in a second, which can be modulated through the `frameRate` variable, to draw the resulting images once its `animate` variable is set to `true`. We can either select to have each resulting image replace the previous one or merge with it using the `clearOnRefresh` variable (its default value is `true`, which means that drawings will be replaced). Then, for a very basic animation, all we need to do is redraw a sprite to a new position every time so that it appears as if it is moving towards some direction. There are two ways to do this: by means of manually calculating what the new coordinates are and by means of using geometrical transformations. In both cases, we need some sort of a *counter* variable that will increment with respect to some unit of time, and we will use it to modulate our sprite's positioning. A readily available counter is the `frame` instance variable of `UserView`, which corresponds to the number of frames that have passed since the animation started. For example:

```
( // A descending circle
var window = Window("a decending circle", 400@400).front;
// create the window
var userView = UserView(window, 450@450) // create the UserView
.background_(Color.white)  // set background color
.animate_(true)  // start animation !
.frameRate_(60)  // set frameRate to 60 frames per second
.drawFunc_({  // callback drawing function
  var counter = userView.frame; // count the number of frames
  var x = 100; // no change in the horizontal axis
  var y = counter % (userView.bounds.height+200);
  // calculate y as the modulo of the passed frames
  Pen.fillColor_(Color.yellow);  // set color to yellow
  Pen.addOval(Rect(x,y-200,200,200));  // create a circle
  Pen.fillStroke;  // draw circle
});
)
```

Notice how we use the `%` (modulo) operation herein to calculate the y coordinate. With modulo, we can easily map an ever-incrementing left operand into the range 0-right-operand-minus-one, which in our case ensures that when our circle goes out of bounds, it will wrap back to its initial positioning. In this way, we can achieve a constantly repeated movement. Note that at each frame, the position of our circle is 1 pixel after the previous one (since `frame` is incremented by one every time). Dividing or multiplying our `counter` to control the difference (in pixels) between every subsequent sprite's position will allow us to change the speed of its motion accordingly. However tempting it may be, it is not a good idea to modulate the frame rate to achieve different speeds. Consider, for instance, what will happen if we have to deal with several objects, all moving at different speeds.

Stop motion is an animation technique wherein objects are made to physically move in small increments between individually photographed frames to create the illusion of movement when these frames are animated.

Animating complex shapes and sprites

Remember the windmills we designed in the previous chapter? In the following code, we are rotating three of them in different ways. For this code to work, we need to evaluate the file holding the windmill's factory definition—be sure to update the path if needed.

```
( // rotating windmills
var window, userView, windmills;
(PathName(thisProcess.nowExecutingPath).pathOnly ++
"9677OS_05_windmill_factory.scd").loadPaths;
// first load the windmill factory
windmills = [ // an array with three windmills
  ~windmillFactory.(100@100,80),
  ~windmillFactory.(300@100,80),
  ~windmillFactory.(500@100,80)
];
window = Window("animation and mouse interaction", 600@200).front;
userView = UserView(window, 600@200).background_(Color.white).animate_
(true).frameRate_(60).drawFunc_({ // setup UserView and callback func
  var speed = 100;   // change this to make rotation faster or slower
  Pen.push;
  // uniform motion
  Pen.rotate( userView.frame/speed, 100, 100);
  // simply use frame count
  windmills[0].draw();
  Pen.pop;
  Pen.push;
  // accelerated motion: back and forth
  Pen.rotate( sin(userView.frame / speed) * 2pi, 300,100);
  // use the sinusoid of frame count
  windmills[1].draw();
  Pen.pop;
  Pen.push;
  // even more accelerated !
  Pen.rotate( tan(userView.frame / speed) * 2pi, 500,100);
  // use the tangent of frame count
  windmills[2].draw();
  Pen.pop;
});
)
```

The preceding code exemplifies how to easily achieve accelerated motion with trigonometric operations, as well as how to imply the existence of some environmental force. Indeed, the windmills look as if they are rotating because of the wind. Note that drawFunc will be evaluated several times in a second; therefore, to optimize the performance, we should ensure that no redundant calculations are performed therein. This is why in the previous chapter, we created a windmill factory in such a way that its construction and initialization stages are separated. If we use a drawing function instead, we will have to perform the same calculations to compute the angular distances between each wing, 60 times per second for every windmill. This would result in unnecessary calculations.

Fundamental animation techniques

By using counters and simple mathematical calculations, we can indeed describe all sorts of movements a sprite of arbitrary complexity may perform over time. Notwithstanding, animation is not limited to only moving the sprites around; quite often actually, we will be looking into implementing certain effects or more complex kinds of motion.

Trailing effects

A typical case is that of adding trailing effects to an animation. If done wisely, trailing effects will make our animations a lot more interesting and organic. We can easily achieve such effects if we merge the current frame with the previous ones rather than replacing them. Consider the following code wherein we set the clearOnRefresh variable to false (to instruct UserView to merge every frame with the previous ones) and use a semitransparent rectangle to dampen the previous contents before actually drawing the new content.

```
( // rotating windmill trailing effect
var window, userView, windmill, speed = 100;
(PathName(thisProcess.nowExecutingPath).pathOnly  ++
"9677OS_05_windmill_factory.scd").loadPaths;
// first load the windmill factory
windmill = ~windmillFactory.(225@225,150); // a new windmill
window = Window("Traling Effect", 450@450).front;
userView = UserView(window,450@450).background_(Color.white).animate_
(true).frameRate_(60).clearOnRefresh_(false).drawFunc_({
  Pen.fillColor_(Color(1,1,1,0.4));   // a transparent white
  Pen.addRect(Rect(0,0,450,450));
  /* create a semi-transparent rectangle to dampen previous contents */
  Pen.fill; // draw rectangle
  Pen.push;
  Pen.rotate( tan(userView.frame / speed) * 2pi, 225, 225);
  // rotating windmill
  windmill.draw();  // draw windmill
  Pen.pop;
});
)
```

Interaction and event-driven programming

For certain applications, we will need to interact with our animations to dynamically change some scenery at will. The generic strategy is to use variables of broader scope inside our `drawFunc` variables, so that we can later access and modify them externally somehow. Departing from the previous example, all we need to do is make sure we change the positioning of our windmill with respect to some x and y variables inside our callback function:

```
windmill.refresh(x@y);
```

We will then use sliders to change the value of x and y respectively, as shown in the following code snippet:

```
EZSlider.new(window,430@40,"x",ControlSpec(0,440),{arg slider; x =
slider.value});

EZSlider.new(window,430@40,"y",ControlSpec(0,440),{arg slider; y =
slider.value});
```

The entire code can be found online with the code bundle of this book. The result is shown in the following screenshot:

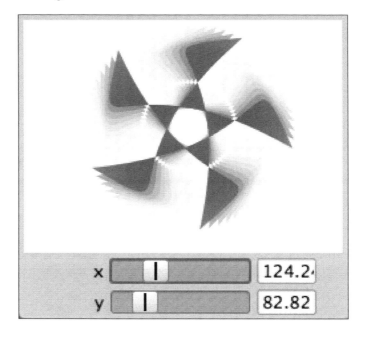

Sometimes we would want to interact not using some GUI but user actions, such as typing through the keyboard, clicking the mouse, resizing a window, or even through some audio signal (we will elaborate on such cases in subsequent chapters). Whenever the flow of a program relies on such user actions, we may speak of **Event-driven Programming (EDP)**. In this programming paradigm, a typical way to associate some user action with a specific task is through *event handlers* that are dedicated callback subroutines, which will perform some task when a particular user action is detected. Dedicated event handlers for a wide range of user actions are already implemented in `UserView` (actually, in any kind of `View`), including moving/dragging/clicking the mouse, using the keyboard, performing drag-and-drop, resizing/moving a `Window` object, and so on. Using event handlers in our context is very similar to using GUI objects as before; the only difference being that we will use the former to modulate our variables. We then need to pass our handler a callback function, which will be evaluated when the corresponding user action is detected with several arguments implicitly passed. These include the parent `View` itself, the handler it is attached to, as well as a number of other arguments relevant to individual user actions; for instance, in the case of `mouseDownAction`, the arguments passed are the *parent* `View`, the cursor's `x` and `y` coordinates, `modifiers` (which modifier keys are in effect, if any), `buttonNumber` (which button is pressed), and `clickCount` (for single, double, or more clicks).

We could easily make the previous example appropriate and use the mouse's cursor to control the positioning of our windmill and mouse clicks to select a new random motion speed (single-click) or a new random density for the trailing effect (double-click). We will have to add the event handlers, as shown in the following code:

```
// event handlers
window.acceptsMouseOver_(true);
// this has to be set to true for the handlers to function properly
userView.mouseDownAction_({arg view, x, y, modifiers,buttonNumber,
clickCount;
  if (clickCount==1) { // on one click
    speed = rrand(10,200); // use this to change speed
  } { // on more clicks
    trailsDensity = rrand(0.1,0.6);
    // change trailing effect's density
  }
});
userView.mouseOverAction_({arg view, x, y; // on mouseOver
  position = x@y;  // use this to change rotation's center
  windmill.refresh(x@y); // change windmill's positioning
});
```

We have to make sure that we declare the variables we need; we update the drawFunc function so that rotation occurs with respect to the new positioning and the speed and trailing effect density are modulated. The entire code can be found online in this book's code bundle. Consider the following screenshot:

Particle systems

Sometimes we would want to set groups of related objects or particle systems in motion. All we need to do is iterate through all of the elements and describe the motion with respect to the iterator's index (or indices) if we want to achieve some sort of interdependent movement. Consider the following code as the departing point:

```
( // animating particles
var particleEngine = { arg width, height, distance, counter;
    (width/distance).floor.do{arg ix;
        (height/distance).floor.do{arg iy;
            var x,y; // positioning
            var color, radius, xoffset, yoffset;

// replace the following as needed
        color = Color.white;
        radius = 30;
        xoffset = 0;
        yoffset = 0;
```

```
        x = (distance/2) + (ix * distance) + xoffset;
        y = (distance/2) + (iy * distance) + yoffset;
        Pen.fillColor_(color);
        Pen.push;
        Pen.rotate(2pi.rand,x,y);
        Pen.addArc(x@y,radius,0,2pi);
        Pen.fill;
        Pen.pop;
    };
  };
};

var window = Window("animating particles", 640@640).front;
var userView = UserView(window, 640@640).background_(Color.black).
animate_(true).frameRate_(60).drawFunc_({
  var counter = userView.frame / 30; // counter
  particleEngine.value(640,640,70,counter);
  // width, height, distance between articles' centers and counter
});
)
```

Now we can simply change the way we calculate radius, color, offset, and counter to achieve various kinds of motion, as shown in the following code:

```
color = Color(sin(counter).abs,cos(counter).abs,sin(counter/4).abs);
  // modulate color
radius = sin(counter / 2).abs * 20; // modulate radius
xoffset = sin(counter) * 10; // move left and right
yoffset = sin(counter/2) * 10; // move up and down
```

Alternatively, to achieve a different kind of motion, we could try the following code:

```
color = Color(sin(ix).abs,cos(ix).abs,sin(iy+ix).abs);
// modulate color
radius = sin((ix+1) * (iy+1) * (counter/10)).abs * 30;
// modulate radius
xoffset = 0;
yoffset = 0;
```

Accelerated motion can be realized by changing the global speed settings as follows:

```
counter = tan(userView.frame / 100).abs;
```

A still from the animation is shown in the following screenshot:

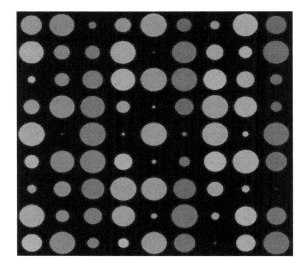

Advanced concepts

More complex animations can be easily generated by means of combining the
fundamental techniques examined previously. Notwithstanding, certain kinds of
motion and certain kinds of structures are impossible to deal with without sufficient
understanding of more advanced concepts—to be touched upon herein. While it is
impossible to scrutinize such specialized topics in depth herein, we will attempt to
have an introduction and give several examples. Readers interested in such topics
may look for more specialized resources.

Animating fractals

As far as fractals are concerned, there are lots of ways in which we can set them in motion. In the following code, for instance, we gradually animate the fractal rather than have all of it drawn at once. The idea is to start with lines of zero length and gradually extend them until the whole fractal is formed. In the fractal factory, we implemented in the previous chapter, we calculated the anchor points of all the line segments the fractal consisted of. Consequently, we already know what the initial and final coordinates for every segment are. All we need to do, then, is use a counter variable that increments from 0 to 1 at certain steps (to be defined by the speed variable) to compute what the ending points for our segments should be for any given frame. Accordingly, we will progressively blend their colors (using the blend instance method of color and with respect to the counter variable) too.

We only need to add a couple of additional variables and an additional animate method to the fractal object we designed in the previous chapter as follows:

```
counter: 0, // counter for animation
animatePoints: Array.newClear(numBranches),
// intermediate points for animation
animate: { arg self, speed = 0.01, colors = [Color.red, Color.green];
  self.branches.do{arg i;
    if (self.counter < 1) { // if not done
      self.counter_(self.counter + speed); // update counter

      // calculate line-segments to draw with respect to counter
      self.animatePoints[i] =
      Point(
        position.x + ((points[i].x - position.x)
          * self.counter),
        position.y + ((points[i].y - position.y)
          * self.counter),
      );

      // draw segment
    Pen.strokeColor_(colors[0].blend(colors[1],self.counter));
    // progressively blend colors with respect to counter
      Pen.line(position,self.animatePoints[i]);
      Pen.stroke;

    } { // if done
```

```
      // draw the completed fractal
      Pen.strokeColor_(colors[0].blend(colors[1],self.counter));
      Pen.line(position,self.animatePoints[i]);
      Pen.stroke;
      self.counter_(0); // reset counter to start from scratch
    };
  };
  // animate children
  if (self.children.notNil) { // if there are children
    // draw all of their branches
    self.children.do{arg item;
      item.animate(speed,colors);
    };
  };
},
```

The full factory can be found in this book's code bundle online. Now we can simply continue as follows:

```
( // fractal animation
var window, userView, fractal;
// first load the fractal factory
(PathName(thisProcess.nowExecutingPath).pathOnly ++
"9677OS_05_07.scd").loadPaths;
window = Window("fractal animation", 640@640).front;
fractal = ~fractalFactory.value(5, 7, window.bounds.center, 60,0.5);
// create a fractal
userView = UserView(window, 640@640).background_(Color.black).animate_
(true).frameRate_(30).drawFunc_({
  fractal.animate(0.001,[Color.red,Color.green]); // animate it
});
)
```

A still frame from the animation is shown in the following screenshot:

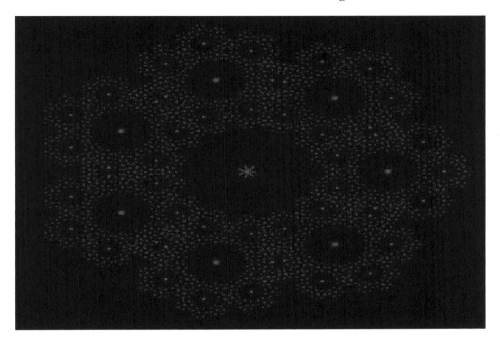

By the way, this is a CPU-demanding example that might cause SuperCollider to crash in weak computers; it is always a good idea to start with fractals of just a few levels and gradually attempt deeper ones to avoid surprises.

Adding dynamics to simulate physical forces

We have already demonstrated how using simple trigonometric functions to achieve accelerated motion implies the presence of wind. We can go further than merely implying physical forces and rather emulate them by means of adding **dynamics** to our animations. Simulating physics can be very tedious and mathematically involved. However, bear in mind that we don't necessarily have to programmatically describe all the laws of physics to have our sprites move in more realistic ways. Actually, we don't even have to be necessarily interested in real-world physics to use dynamics; we may as well want to create our own systems by means of defining non-real-world physical rules specific to the latter. In any case, we can programmatically describe physics and cast the motion behavior accordingly. This can be done by means of defining the individual physical forces that affect a scenery as well as the individual physical properties of every structure that is affected. The latter modulates how the former affects a body. For example, a bouncing ball may be affected by gravity and wind acceleration (physical forces), but it does so explicitly because of their mass and flex. To successfully emulate the behavior of such an object, we merely need to calculate their new positioning with respect to those forces and qualities. However, before actually doing so, we need to familiarize ourselves with vectors.

Certain quantities, such as weight, mass, or flex, have magnitude alone and, consequently, can be described by some simple number. Such quantities are broadly referred to as **scalars**. Forces, however, are not scalars as they typically have both magnitude and direction. Consider for example, acceleration, velocity, or pressure; none of those forces can be described simply with a number. Such quantities are referred to as **vectors** in physics. In a computer graphics context, a vector is a complex mathematical entity characterized by both magnitude and a direction. The easiest way to conceptualize a vector is as an n-dimensional arrow pointing at a certain direction and having its origin at the center (whatever it may stand for) of the structure that is affected. Then, any force can be represented as a set of n-dimensional Cartesian co-ordinates representing the point at the end of that arrow minus its origin (which is usually considered as the zero point for simplicity). Relying on vector algebra, we can calculate what the overall effect of individually applied forces would be on some form. In the following figure, for example, we can see towards what direction a body would move if we apply to it three vectors: P(2,0,0), P(0,3,0), and P(0,0,5). The result is P(2,3,5).

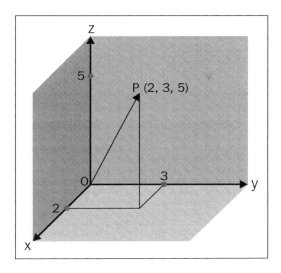

The significant advantage of using vectors is that we will not have to perform all these calculations ourselves but rather rely on appropriate methods of some vector object. While there is no built support for vectors in SuperCollider, there is indeed a `Quark` extension, namely VectorSpace, which provides us with miscellaneous vector classes we can use to represent vectors and perform all major algebraic operations on vectors. The following code exemplifies how we can use `RealVector3D` (`RealVector2D` is similar in spirit).

```
a = RealVector3D[1,2,3]; // create a new 3d vector
a.x; // access first coefficient
a.y; // access second coefficient
a.z; // access third coefficient
a = a * RealVector3D[pi,2.4,3]; // multiply it with another
```

Now we will use vectors to emulate how a ball would bounce in the presence of various forces such as gravity, wind, and friction, and with respect to its mass and flex. We will start by designing a model for the ball. We need variables for position, mass and flex, as well as velocity and acceleration. We will also need an `addForce` method that will first normalize the force added with respect to the ball's `mass` and then calculate what the ball's `acceleration` should be with respect to this normalized force. We can later have our ball affected by as many forces as we want (using `addForce`) and have the ball's `acceleration` updated accordingly. Afterwards, we need a `draw` method that will calculate the current ball's `velocity` with respect to `acceleration`, compute what the ball's positioning should be, and draw it accordingly. Its bouncing behavior is implemented inside `draw` using `if` structures. The ball will bounce whenever it encounters any of our canvas' edges with respect to its `flex`; some of its `acceleration` should also be lost due to friction as shown in the following code:

```
(// a ball factory
~ballFactory = { arg radius=40, initialPosition=0@0, color=Color.
green, mass=10, flex=0.9, bounds;
// the bounds define when the ball should bounce
  var ball = (
    velocity: RealVector3D[0,0,0],        // initial velocity
    mass: mass,    // the mass of the ball
    flex: flex,    // 1 is perfectly non-elastic and 0 perfectly elastic
    position: initialPosition,  // position of the ball
    acceleration: RealVector3D[0,0,0],
    // acceleration of the movement
    addForce: { arg self,force;    // add forces to the ball
      var normalizedForce;
      normalizedForce = force * self.mass;
      // force should be affected by the mass
      self.acceleration_(self.acceleration + normalizedForce);
      // calculate acceleration
    },
    draw: {arg self;  // draw ball
      self.velocity_(self.velocity + self.acceleration); // calculate
current velocity
      self.acceleration_(RealVector3D[0,0]); // reset acceleration
      self.position_(self.position + self.velocity);
      /* calculate new position - we can indeed add a RealVector2D
      with a point ! */
      // make ball bounce
      if (self.position.y > bounds.y) {
        self.velocity[1] = self.velocity[1].neg * self.flex;
        self.position.y = bounds.y;
      };
```

```
          if (self.position.y < 1) {
            self.velocity[1] = self.velocity[1].neg * self.flex;
            self.position.y = 1;
          };
          if ((self.position.x > bounds.x) || (self.position.x < 1)) {
            self.velocity[0] = self.velocity[0].neg * self.flex;
          };
          Pen.fillColor_(color);
          Pen.addArc(self.position,radius,0,2pi);
          Pen.fill;
        }
      );
    ball;
  };
)
```

Now we can proceed as follows:

```
( // bouncing balls example
var window, userView, ball; // window, userView and ball
var wind, gravity, frictionX, frictionY; // various forces

// first load the ball factory
(PathName(thisProcess.nowExecutingPath).pathOnly ++
"9677OS_05_10.scd").loadPaths;

window = Window("bouncing ball", 640@640).front;
userView = UserView(window, 640@640).background_(Color.black).animate_
(true).frameRate_(60).drawFunc_({
  if ((userView.frame % 240) == 0) { // every 4 seconds (4 x 60frames)

    // create a ball of random characteristics
    var mass = rrand(5,15);
    var flex = rrand(0.7,1.0).trunc(0.1);
    ball = ~ballFactory.(radius:40,
      initialPosition:Point(rrand(0,400),0),
      color:Color.rand, mass:mass, flex:flex,
      bounds: 640@640);
    ("New ball of mass" + mass + "and of flex" + flex + "created").
      postln;
    // create random forces
    wind = RealVector3D[rrand(0.01,0.3).trunc(0.01),rrand(0.01,0.3).
    trunc(0.01),rrand(0,0.3).trunc(0.01)];
    // wind from some random direction
```

```
        gravity = RealVector3D[0,0.4,0]; // gravity is always 0.8
        frictionX = RealVector3D[0.1,0,0]; // horizontal friction
        frictionY = RealVector3D[0,0.1,0]; // vertical friction
        ("Forces applied are: Wind," + wind + "Gravity," + gravity +
          "Horizontal Friction," + frictionX + "Verical Friction" +
          frictionY).postln;
    };

    // add forces to the ball
    ball.addForce(wind);
    ball.addForce(gravity);
    if ((ball.position.x > 640) || (ball.position.x < 1)) {
      // if touching horizontal edges apply horizontal friction
      ball.addForce(frictionX);
    } { // else if touching the bottom apply vertical friction
      if (ball.position.y == 640);
      ball.addForce(frictionY);
    };

    ball.draw(); // draw the ball
  });
  )
```

Kinematics

Hitherto, we have only dealt with monolithic sprites that move as a whole towards some direction. But what if the body we want to set in motion is articulated? Therein, we would have to calculate what the new position should be for each one of its parts according to its intrinsic rules. And in fact, how can we model articulated bodies that behave organically? To deal with such cases, we must resort to **kinematics**, which is the study of how mechanical points, bodies, and systems of bodies move. Herein, we will attempt a demonstration of how we can model and move an articulated snake-like creature. Our snake will consist of line segments of gradually decrementing width, each of which will be able to bend up to a certain angle. Then we need to describe programmatically how every segment should move when the whole body is asked to move towards some arbitrary direction. We will have a variable (named theta) constantly incremented by a small number so that the tail of the snake has the tendency to move and then have every movement of the head back-propagate accordingly. This is done by means of computing what the position of each segment should be as a function of simple trigonometric operations and with respect to the positioning of the adjacent ones. A snake factory is given herein. Notice that the color argument should be a function and that it will be implicitly passed an index incrementing from 0 to 1. We can use this to create smooth color progressions and gradients as shown in the following code:

```
( // a kinematic snake factory
~snakeFactory = { arg numberOfSegments = 50, length = 20,  width = 40,
colorFunc = {arg i; Color(1,0,i)};

  // the body
  var body =  Array.fill(numberOfSegments, {arg i;
    (position: 0@(i * 2), radius: (2 * (50 - i) / 2)); // an event
  });

  var snake = ( // the snake
    position: 0@0, // the current position of the sname
    theta: 0.1, // used to calculate the angles
    draw: { arg self;
      self.theta_(self.theta + 0.0005); // increment theta

      body[0].position_(self.position); // the position of the head
      body[1].position_(Point(body[0].position.x + sin( pi + self.
      theta), body[0].position.y + cos( pi + self.theta).neg));
      // the next to the head segment is calculated as a function of
      theta

      /* calculate the position and color of each segment with respect
      to the adjacent ones */
      (numberOfSegments-4).do{ arg i;
      /* iterate over the rest segments (-4 because we access i+2,i+1
        and i herein) */
        var newPosition, hypotenuse, points;
        var index = i + 2;
        var color = colorFunc.(index/numberOfSegments);
        // calculate color
        newPosition = body[index].position - body[index-2].position;
        // calculate the new position as a function of a previous
        segment's position

        hypotenuse = newPosition.x.hypot(newPosition.y);
        // calculate the hypotenuse between x and y of this new
        position
        body[index].position_( body[index-1].position + ((newPosition
        * length) / hypotenuse)); // set the positioning of this snake

        points = [
        // array with the positions of 2 consecutive segments
          body[index-1].position,
          body[index].position
        ];

        // draw segment
        Pen.strokeColor_(color);
        Pen.width_(width*(numberOfSegments-index)/numberOfSegments);
        Pen.line(points[0],points[1]);
```

```
        Pen.stroke();
      };
    },
    refresh: { arg self, newPosition;
      self.position_(newPosition); // update position
    }
  );

  snake;
};
)
```

Then, we can use the model as shown in the following code:

```
( // kinematics example
var window, userView, snake;
// first load the snake factory
(PathName(thisProcess.nowExecutingPath).pathOnly ++
"9677OS_05_12.scd").loadPaths;
snake = ~snakeFactory.(50,20,40);
window = Window("Kinematic snake", 640@640).front.acceptsMouseOver_
(true); // to enable mouse actions
userView = UserView(window, 640@640).background_(Color.black).animate_
(true).frameRate_(60).drawFunc_({
  snake.draw;
});
userView.mouseOverAction_({arg m,x,y;
  snake.refresh(x@y);
});
)
```

A screenshot is shown as follows:

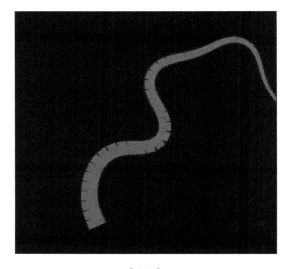

Summary

In this chapter, we discussed animation and elaborated on both basic and more advanced techniques. These include animating monolithic shapes and sprites, implementing interaction and trailing effects, emulating the effect of environmental forces, and setting in motion particle systems, fractals, and articulated bodies.

In the next chapter, we will learn how to retrieve data from various sources, including off-line and online databases as well as by means of analyzing audio signals; we'll also learn how to manipulate and preprocess data and perform data mappings and encodings.

6
Data Acquisition and Mapping

In the previous two chapters, we dealt with computer-generated graphics and the various ways to achieve animation, thus preparing the groundwork for designing more sophisticated data/audio visualizers. Doing so, however, also involves retrieving, manipulating, and encoding data appropriately, which will be discussed in this chapter. More to the point, we will examine various mechanisms to acquire and generate data from a wide range of possible sources, as well as the methodologies to process, encode, and distribute them within our programs. Such techniques are invaluable in miscellaneous contexts, and even if at this point they appear largely irrelevant with visualization, they are rather fundamental to it and are encountered even in the simplest scenarios. Readers primarily interested in the latter will have to be patient during this chapter; all will make sense in the next one.

The topics that will be covered in this chapter are as follows:

- Retrieving data from local or remote databases
- Using OSC and serial communication protocols
- Machine listening and audio information retrieval
- Testing and preprocessing data
- Basic mappings and encodings
- Exchanging data within our programs

Data acquisition

These days, data is literally everywhere: stored on local or remote databases, accessed through dedicated Application Programming Interfaces (APIs), distributed through File Transfer Protocol (FTP), and even generated dynamically by specialized hardware or software. Data acquisition stands for those techniques involved in acquiring the already existent data, and is not to be confused with the relevant, albeit fundamentally different, tasks of *information retrieval* or *feature extraction*. The latter refer to generating or extracting (otherwise nonexistent) information by means of analyzing data. In all cases, to import data in SuperCollider we need a source and a channel, the former being the place where the data of interest happens to be at, and the latter being the way to retrieve the data.

An **Application Programming Interface** specifies how certain software components are to be accessed extrinsically and how they are supposed to interact with each other.

A **File Transfer Protocol** is a network protocol used to transfer files from one host to another and is typically used on the Internet.

Dealing with local files

The most fundamental of all data acquisition techniques is how to read from or write to some local file, or in other words, how to perform file I/O (that is, input and output) operations. The reason is that quite often, we can simplify more complex data acquisition problems if we simply use local files as intermediates. In SuperCollider, all file I/O tasks are addressed through the `File` class. Writing data to a file is very easy:

1. Open the file for either writing (using the `"w"` keyword or the `"wb"` keyword for the binary files) or for appending (using the `"a"` keyword or the `"ab"` keyword for the binary files).

2. Invoke `write` with our dataset as an argument.

When in writing mode, a new file will be created, replacing already existent ones having the same name (there is no way to undo this so we should be careful). In appending mode, a new file will be created too, but this time if there is an already existent one with the same name, then data will be appended to its end. A simple example follows:

```
( // storing data to a local file
var data = Array.fill(1000,{rrand(0,1000)});
// an array of random values
var file = File("dataset.dat".absolutePath,"w");
// open for writing operations
data.do{ arg i;
  file.write(i + "\n");
// write data adding new line character to the end
};
file.close;  // close file when done
)
```

Note that we have to add some kind of delimiter (a newline in this case) between each piece of data if we want to be able to distinguish between entries later; otherwise, each datum would stick next to each other, in this case resulting in a single number of 1000 digits. We can use the absolutePath (or the standardizePath) method to resolve ~ (which stands for the home directory in POSIX (that is, Unix-like) operating systems and which is incomprehensible to Microsoft Windows) to a proper path (which in my case is /Users/Marinos/). If we only provide it with a filename instead of a full path, our new file will be created in the default directory, which is in the folder wherein SuperCollider is installed. Then, to read the contents of our newly generated file we can use the readAllString method:

```
( // read a file
var file = File("dataset.dat".absolutePath,"r");
// open for reading operations
var data = file.readAllString;
data.postln;
file.close;  // close file when done
)
```

Apparently this method will read the files as a single `String` object. This approach, however, can be problematic for several reasons. The major drawback with this way is that we merely copy the contents of the whole file to our computer's memory, which could be easily overloaded if large datasets are read. When dealing with large datasets or with datasets of unknown sizes, it is wiser to read chunks of data one at a time instead. We can do so using the `getLine`, `getChar`, or `getFloat` methods (depending on what kind of data we need to retrieve) within some routine, for example:

```
( // reading chunks of data
var file, data;
file = File("~/dataset.dat".absolutePath,"r");
 // open for reading operations
fork{loop{ // use a routine to read a chunk at a time
  if (file.pos != file.length) { // if there are data left
    data = file.getLine; // get a new line of data
    data.postln; // do something with data
  } {  // close file and stop routine when done
    "done !".postln;
    file.close;
    thisThread.stop;
  };
  0.01.wait;  // wait before iterating through the remaining data
}};
)
```

Every open file is associated with an implicit variable indicating the position in the file from where the next value will be read. This position pointer starts at 0 and increments accordingly every time we access the data. In this example, we use `pos` to access this variable and test it against the total `length` value of the file to stop when we have read all data. It is worth mentioning too, that but for having used a newline (that is, \n) delimiter before, we wouldn't be able to use the `getLine` method in this example. Generally speaking, it is of great importance to know how the contents of a file are structured before attempting to read them. Most kinds of files containing data follow the convention of beginning with some sort of header (that is, a string of text giving information on the kind of data, and so on) followed by the data entries separated by some kind of delimiter. Regarding the header, we may want to read it and have our algorithm configured accordingly, or we can totally ignore it (by simply omitting the first line) if we already know what kind of data we are dealing with. As far as delimiters are concerned, the most common ones are tabs, commas, semicolons, new lines, or spaces. We have already demonstrated how to get the next entry when data are delimited with the new lines. There are also specialized file readers available for other kinds of delimiters namely, `TabFileReader`, `SemiColonFileReader`, `CSVFileReader` (**CSV** stands for **Comma Separated Values**), or the generic `FileReader` delimiter which can be instructed to identify any kind of delimiter. For example:

```
( // using custom delimiters
var data = Array.fill(1000,{rrand(0,1000)});
// an array of random values
var file = File("dataset.dat".absolutePath,"w");
// open for writing operations
data.do{ arg item;
  file.write(item.asString + $@);
// write data adding a custom delimiter
};
file.close;  // close file when done
// read data with FileRead
data = FileReader.read("dataset.dat".absolutePath,delimiter: $@);
data[0].postln; // print data in the post window
)
```

Note that `FileReader.read` will return a 2D array wherein each entry represents data found on each line. In our case, all of our data are placed consecutively in a single line, therefore all of them are to be found in the first entry of the result.

Accessing data remotely

Cases that involve accessing data from some remote location are probably the norm rather than the exception these days, be it via the World Wide Web, FTP, or some private host. Our basic approach is to first download the corresponding file locally and then proceed as before. We can programmatically download files locally by means of some third-party command-line utility and SuperCollider's shell support. A **shell** is a command-line interface for an operating system, and as such it will respect different kinds of commands depending on what our platform is. In this book, I assume a POSIX operating system, such as Mac OS X or some flavor of Linux, albeit most of these commands are compatible with Windows too, with no or with minor modifications. Shell support in SuperCollider is implemented through a set of dedicated methods of the `String` class, namely, `unixCmd` (execute a command asynchronously, that is, without waiting for it to finish before our program advances), `systemCmd` (execute a command synchronously, that is, to wait for it to finish before continuing), `unixCmdGetStdOut` (execute a command synchronously and return the output), and `unixCmdGetStdOutLines` (execute a command synchronously and store each line of the output into an `Array` object).

As far as the third-party utility is concerned, there are many options, the most famous of which are probably *wget* and *curl*. We will use the latter tool hereinafter which, if not already installed, can be download from `http://curl.haxx.se/download.html` (binaries exist for most major operating systems). Curl will print the contents of the file in **stdout** (that is, the standard output, which is typically our screen) or write them to a file if a `-o` flag and a filename are specified. Consider the following example, wherein we download a file from a remote server containing comma-separated numerical data and then read it into an array:

```
( // accessing remotely stored data with curl
var data, path;
path = "arrhythmia.data".absolutePath; // destination path
("curl \"http://archive.ics.uci.edu/ml/machine-learning-databases/
arrhythmia/arrhythmia.data\" -o" + path).systemCmd;
"ok reading !".postln;
data = CSVFileReader.read("arrhythmia.data".absolutePath,true,true);
)
```

This particular dataset is multidimensional, contains cardiac arrhythmia measurements, and is freely available on the Internet in plain text format. If our file was HTML formatted, we could use the `readAllStringHTML` method of `File` instead, to strip it out of all code and only keep the actual text.

There are also cases, wherein we can only access data through some dedicated API. The website `http://www.random.org` offers on demand true (emphasis added) random numbers that are generated using measurements of atmospheric noise. To get the numbers we have to use its specialized HTML API to describe how many and what kind of numbers we want; details on that particular API can be found at `http://www.random.org/clients/http/`. In the following example, we demand 52 random integers in plain text format:

```
( // accessing remote data from random.org
var data = "curl \"http://www.random.org/sequences/?min=1&max=52&col=1
&format=plain&rnd=new\" ".unixCmdGetStdOutLines;
data.postln;
)
```

In this particular case wherein the API is an HTML interface, all we had to do is use curl as before, but with a properly formatted HTTP address this time. In other cases, we might have to use some other kind of utility or programming environment to access the data. Afterwards, depending on what particular tools we use, we may either store the data to some file and then read them in SuperCollider, use shell support to read them from the standard output, or send them to SuperCollider via one of the supported communication protocols, as to be discussed promptly.

Using OSC

There are cases wherein we need to establish real-time communication with SuperCollider and a third-party software or hardware; for example, when data is generated on the fly elsewhere or when we rely on some specialized API which will send data asynchronously. **Open Sound Control** (**OSC**) is currently the most significant communication protocol, being highly optimized for modern networking technology, accurate, fast, and highly customizable. If the hardware/software we are interested in bridging with SuperCollider supports it, this is the protocol to be used. By the way, all of the SuperCollider's internal language/server communication is also built on OSC. Before discussing OSC's messaging style, we need to discuss how to establish communication between the various parts involved.

OSC protocol is based upon the so-called **User Datagram Protocol** (**UDP**), which is a purely network-oriented protocol. Hence, we have to first set up a network and establish communication with the other end, even if it is just an application in the same computer. The sender has to be configured to send OSC messages to that Internet Protocol (IP) address and to the port that the SuperCollider language (SCLang) is listening to. As far as the *port* is concerned, the default is 57120, but we can always evaluate `NetAddr.langPort` just to double-check it. The situation is a bit more complicated as far as IP addresses are concerned. If communication is about to occur only within our computer, then we can simply use `127.0.0.1`, which is our local IP address. If we want to communicate with some device in our local network, that is, directly connected to our computer or to the same router we are connected with, we need to find out our *internal IP address*, using some utility such as `ifconfig` (in POSIX systems) or `ipconfig` (in Windows); in my computer if I evaluate `"ifconfig".unixCmd`, I get several lines of text, some of which are:

```
en1: flags=8863<UP,BROADCAST,SMART,RUNNING,SIMPLEX,MULTICAST>mtu 1500
    ether 00:26:bb:09:16:09
    inet6 fe80::226:bbff:fe09:1609%en1 prefixlen 64 scopeid 0x5
    inet 192.168.10.9 netmask 0xffffff00 broadcast 192.168.10.255
    media: autoselect
    status: active
```

Therefore my internal IP address is `192.168.10.9`. If communication is to be established between remote clients outside our local network, for instance with some webserver or with some computer in a geographically different location, we need to find out our *external IP address*. This we cannot do locally, since our operating system is unaware of it. We rather have to use some service such as `http://ip.alt.io/` and `http://www.whatismyip.com/`. Bear in mind, however, that both the internal and external IP addresses will most likely change when we reboot our router or when we disconnect and reconnect to the network. There are ways to guarantee a static IP address if needed for critical applications (the easiest, but not free way, is to ask one from our Internet Service Provider (ISP); another alternative would be to use Dynamic DNS services and configure our router accordingly, note that several ISPs consider this a violation of the contract).

Thereafter, we need to register an `OSCFunc` object to schedule something to happen when the desired message arrives. Such kinds of objects are referred to as responders. We can configure our responder to only listen to the messages arriving from a particular IP address, port, or to a particular kind of message, passing the appropriate arguments. As for ports, we need to clarify that the sender's port is the one from which messages are dispatched, and that this is not (necessarily) the same port to which we are sending the messages. `OSCFunc` detects the former, rather than the latter, which can be found either by consulting the specifications of the third-party software/hardware we are using or by means of evaluating `OSCFunc.trace`. The latter will print detailed information on all the incoming OSC messages in the post window, wherein we can also see the sender's IP address and port number, as well as the very message itself. Note that the server tends to send a lot of OSC messages to the SCLang if the former is active; so we shouldn't be surprised if we witness a lot of messages that we didn't send.

Having established a communication channel, we can start sending OSC messages to SuperCollider. The latter are identified by their path, which is a string of keywords that are separated by slashes, for instance `"/msg/test"`. To register a responder for this message, we can simply:

```
( // respond to an incoming OSC message
OSCFunc({ arg msg;
  msg.postln;  // print the message bundle
},'/msg/test'); // listen to /msg/test message
)
```

The actual body of an OSC message may consist of an arbitrary number of characters. We can also send `Arrays` but they have to consist of 8-bit integers only. We can test our responder within SuperCollider as follows:

```
( // send an OSC message to the Client
var receiver = NetAddr.new("127.0.0.1", 57120); // localhost
var data = Int8Array.fill(100,{rrand(0,100)}); // 8bit data
receiver.sendMsg("/msg/test", data); // send OSC message
)
```

It has to be stressed that the UDP protocol does not check whether our data has arrived intact or not, therefore it is not a good strategy to send large datasets at once via OSC because if they never arrive we might not be able to tell. Possible solutions to these problems are either sending chunks of data, so that even if some messages never arrive the cost is bearable or implementing a custom communication system ourselves, wherein the responder will reply to the sender once it has received a message and the latter will wait for the receiver's confirmation before advancing to the next message. Depending on the context, even more sophisticated communication could be implemented, wherein each message sent would also contain information on its unique ID and the number of chunks remaining, so that the receiver could keep track of everything and explicitly ask for a particular chunk if it never arrived.

UDP, designed by *David Reed* in 1980, is one of the core network protocols used for the Internet, which allows computer applications to send messages to other hosts without having to explicitly set up special transmission channels beforehand.

Internet Protocol address is a numerical label assigned to each device participating in a computer network that uses the Internet Protocol for communication.

Using MIDI

The **Musical Instrument Digital Interface** (**MIDI**) is reminiscent of the 80s, but still remains the protocol of choice for several software or hardware manufacturers. In my opinion, it is both unfortunate and sad that certain contemporary pieces of software or hardware only support MIDI and not OSC, nevertheless this is a scenario encountered quite often these days, so we must be fluent with MIDI as well. Bear in mind that using MIDI is our only option when we need to communicate with outdated hardware synthesizers, computers, and relevant equipment that were created before OSC was standardized. When compared to OSC, MIDI is a very limited protocol. The kinds of messages we can send are very specific, namely, *note on messages* (comprising of a MIDI note number and a velocity value), *note off* messages, *control change* messages (comprising of a controller number and its new value), and *program change* messages (to change a device's patch). Other specialized kinds of MIDI may be encountered too, such as **System exclusive** (**SysEx**), which are device specific and follow no definite standard, as well as various kinds of timing messages such as MIDI Time Code (MTC) or Society of Motion Picture and Television Engineers (SMPTE) time code. Indicative of MIDI's limitations is that, as far as the standard messages are concerned, all data sent has to be in the range of 0-127 (7 bits).

To communicate via MIDI we need to physically connect some MIDI capable device to our computer via either DIN-5 cables and some specialized MIDI interface for older hardware, or USB for more recent devices. When only software is concerned, we have to rely on some software utility to create and configure a virtual MIDI path between SuperCollider and the application in question. Listening to MIDI messages in SuperCollider is addressed by the MIDIFunc class either through the generic *new method or the specific *cc, *noteOn, *noteOff, *sysEx, *program, *smpte, and *mtcQuarterFrame methods. The MIDI protocol defines 16 discrete channels of communication. Both MIDI-capable hardware and software are typically configured to send messages either to a particular one or to all of them. Likewise, we can setup an instance of MIDIFunc to listen to all channels or to some in particular and furthermore, we can configure it to only respond to messages coming from a particular node by supplying its unique source ID. As with OSCFunc, there is a *trace method available which we can use to monitor all incoming messages and find out the specifics of an individual sender. The following code registers MIDI responders for control change and system exclusive messages:

```
( // registering MIDI responders
MIDIIn.connectAll; // connect incoming ports
MIDIFunc.cc({arg value, ccNumber; // listen to control change messages
  "Control Change message received !".postln;
  [value, ccNumber].postln;
  // do sth with the value and the controller's number
```

```
}, nil);
/* nil stands for listening to any cc message coming from everywhere */
MIDIFunc.sysex({arg data; // listen to sysex messages
  "System Exclusive received !".postln;
  [data].postln;  // do sth with the message
},nil); // listen to any message coming from everywhere
)
```

SysEx messages are of particular interest, as they are the only kind of MIDI messages we can use to send packets of data. Such packets should always start with the hexadecimal number `0xf0` and end with the hexadecimal number `0xf7`. We can test the previous responders from within SuperCollider. Firstly, we need to make sure that some virtual MIDI port is installed and enabled on our computer. Then we can try the following code:

```
( // sending MIDI messages
var midi, data, sysExPacket;
midi = MIDIOut(0); // assuming a virtual midi port at index 0
midi.control(10,34,124); // send 124 at cc34 channel 10
data = Int8Array.fill(15,{rrand(0,100)}); // generate data
sysExPacket = data.insert(0,0xf0).add(0xf7); // format data as sysEx
midi.sysex(sysExPacket); // send a syxEx packet
)
```

Using Serial Port

It may be that we want to retrieve the data from some microcontroller or other specialized hardware over some serial computer bus. How to do so largely depends on the kind of hardware we want to interface with, yet there does exists a generic `SerialPort` class. We first need to connect our hardware to our computer and identify what its serial bus is by invoking `SerialPort.listDevices`; then, we can proceed as follows:

```
( // reading bytes from some serial bus
var port = SerialPort( /* port path here */, baudrate: 9600, crtscts:
true /* enable hardware data flow control */);
fork{5.do{ // read 5 next bytes
  port.next.postln; // read next byte
  1.wait; // wait 1 second;
}};
SerialPort.closeAll; // close all ports when done;
)
```

Of course, the **baud rate** (that is, the rate of dataflow) we have set must match that of the hardware we use. In the case of the famous (at least in the DIY circles) Arduino series of microcontroller-based prototyping boards, there are specialized quarks already available that we can use instead of the `SerialPort` class namely, `Arduino` or `SCPyduino`. An example with the latter (remember to install it first) would look as follows:

```
( // polling data from Arduino
var arduino, loop;
// connect on given port and baud rate set to 57600
arduino = SCPyduino.new("/dev/tty.usbmodem411", 57600);
arduino.analog[0].active_(1); // activate polling on Analog pin 0
loop = fork{1000.do{ // read 1000 bytes from arduino
  arduino.iterate; // sync with arduino's clock
  arduino.analog[0].value; // do sth with data read
}};
arduino.close; // close when done
)
```

In this example, the `"/dev/tty.usbmodem411"` parameter is our device's path and `57600` is the baud rate we have used. In order to make this code work, we also need to load the *StandardFirmata* example code in our Arduino, which we can find in the **Examples | Firmata** submenu of the Arduino **Integrating Development Environment** (IDE), which in this case is the Arduino software we have downloaded from www.arduino.cc. We also have to make sure that the baud rate used in *StandardFirmata* does indeed match ours in SuperCollider. **Firmata** is a specialized library designed for fast and efficient communication with microcontrollers such as Arduino. The Arduino Quark achieves communication via the standard Serial console instead.

An Integrated Development Environment is an application targeting the software developers and providing them with relevant facilities such as a source code editor, build automation tools, an interpreter, and a debugger.

Machine listening

So far we've examined in detail how we can acquire data from various sources. In a visualization context, however, we may encounter situations wherein we will need to control some elements of an animation with respect to some particular characteristic of a signal, for example, their amplitude or their frequency. Yet, these kinds of information are attributes of the signal, rather than parts of it. In other words, we need something to happen not with respect to some existent data (that is, our signal in this context) but with respect to certain characteristics of a data flow. Consider that an audio signal is completely unaware of how loud it is or of what its frequency is. Remember that audio signals are merely streams of numbers and that sounds are merely fluctuations of air pressure. The reason we understand sounds as having loudness or pitch, is because our auditory apparatus analyzes them and provides the brain with information on certain sonic qualities. Further, more sophisticated perceptua and cognitive processes perform additional kinds of analyses to extract as well as attribute information and meanings, so that we perceptually decipher what we hear. Likewise, we can say that a signal is periodic and has a certain frequency, only if we somehow analyze it. Remember that the output of a sinusoidal wave at a frequency of 200 Hz is just a flow of numbers between ±1. The datum 200 is not part of this signal, so the only way to make something happen with respect to this number is to actually generate it by means of analyzing the audio signal against its frequency. The task of retrieving statistical and other kinds of information from audio signals is generally referred to as **machine listening**.

Machine listening is, in essence, to analyze signals in order to generate information that represent certain qualities of these signals. To properly understand and evaluate the kind of information we may get from some machine listening algorithm, it is worth distinguishing briefly the different kinds of properties a signal may have. Acoustic properties refer to physical properties of sound, and consequently of audio signals, particularly qualities such as *amplitude*, frequency, and *spectrum*. Psychoacoustic properties refer to low-level perceptional properties of audio signals, such as *loudness*, *pitch*, and *timbre*. Psychoacoustic properties are fundamentally different than their acoustic equivalents, the latter being intrinsically linked to perception. For instance, loudness refers to how loud something sounds, while the amplitude stands for the actual amount of the displacement of the air particles that occurs in the physical space. It has to be stressed that the various psychoacoustic qualities do relate and depend upon the acoustic properties of sound; nonetheless, the relationships are very complex and not that straightforward as they may appear to be. For example, loudness does not depend exclusively upon amplitude, but it also depends upon frequency, spectral content, and even upon a series of psychological and other factors. We can also speak of several families of higher-level perceptional properties, such as musical ones (*scale*, *tonality*, *rhythm*, *genre*, *expressivity*, and so on), cognitive ones (semantics, symbolical signification, and so on), and psychological ones (irritability, entertainability, ability to cause relaxation, and so on). Again, such properties may depend or relate to some extent to the acoustic or psychoacoustic qualities of sound; yet the inter-relationships may be extremely complex and even not fully understood in certain cases.

Machine listening algorithms are not limited only to simple acoustic properties of a signal; sophisticated algorithms have been proposed for more complex problems as well such as musical style recognition and rhythm extraction. As far as musical qualities are concerned, the more specialized term musical information retrieval is sometimes encountered too. In SuperCollider we can easily perform basic audio analyses to retrieve information on both physical as well as certain perceptional properties of audio signals using the available machine listening UGens, the most important of which will be discussed immediately.

 Music Information Retrieval (MIR) is an interdisciplinary field of science dealing with how to retrieve and classify information from music.

Tracking amplitude and loudness

In *Chapter 1, Scoping, Plotting, and Metering,* we briefly demonstrated how to use the `Amplitude` UGen to track peak amplitude linearly. We can also use the `Peak` UGen, which will return the maximum peak amplitude every time it receives a trigger or the `PeakFollower` UGen which smoothly decays from the maximum value by some specified decay time. To track the minimum or the maximum value of a signal we can use the `RunningMin` or `RunningMax` UGens. To track Root Mean Square (RMS) amplitude, we can use the `RunningSum` UGen. The following example shows how to use these UGens:

```
(// tracking amplitude
{   var sound = SinOsc.ar(mul:LFNoise2.kr(1).range(0,1)); // source
    RunningSum.rms(sound,100).poll(label:'rms'); // rms
    Amplitude.kr(sound).poll(label:'peak'); // peak
    Peak.kr(sound, Impulse.kr(1)).poll(label:'peak_trig');
    // peak when triggered
    PeakFollower.kr(sound).poll(label:'peak_dec'); // peak with decay
    RunningMin.kr(sound).poll(label:'min'); // minimum
    RunningMax.kr(sound).poll(label:'max'); // maximum
    Out.ar(0,sound); // write to output
}.play;
)
```

Sometimes we may want something to happen when a signal is silent or at least when it is below a certain level. In such cases we can use `DetecteSilence`. There also exists a `Loudness` UGent which will estimate loudness in **Sones** (the measure of loudness). It is designed to analyze spectra and requires an FFT window of size 1024 for sampling rates of 44100 or 48000 and of the size 2048 for 88200 or 96000, respectively. For example:

```
( // track loudness
{   var sound, loudness;
    sound = SinOsc.ar(LFNoise2.ar(1).range(100,10000),
        mul:LFNoise0.ar(1).range(0,1)); // source
    loudness = FFT(LocalBuf(1024),sound); // sampling rates of 44.1/48K
    // loudness = FFT(LocalBuf(1024),sound);
    // sampling rates of 88.2/96K
    loudness = Loudness.kr(loudness).poll(label:\loudness);
    Out.ar(0, sound);
}.play;
)
```

Tracking frequency

As far as frequency is concerned, there are a number of relevant UGens, each of them implemented differently. The most simple one is ZeroCrossing, which will estimate the frequency by keeping track of how often an input signal crosses the horizontal axis, which represents 0 in terms of amplitude. Pitch is a more accurate frequency tracker, which also allows for some tweaking. Note that, regardless of its name, it performs frequency tracking rather than pitch tracking, the latter also depending on a series of other factors. More advanced frequency trackers are Tartini (which is based on the method used in the homonymous open source pitch tracker) and Qitch (which has to be used along with one of the special auxiliary WAV files it is distributed with). Tartini and Qitch are not included in the standard SuperCollider distribution but on the SC3Plugins extension bundle (available at http://sc3-plugins.sourceforge.net/). Pitch, Tartini, and Qitch will all return an array of instances of OutProxy obtaining both the estimated frequency as well as a flag of 1 or 0 to denote whether they successfully tracked some frequency or not. When attempting to track frequency we should always bear in mind that the former being a complicated process, not all trackers would work equally well for all kinds of signals. For example:

```
( // frequency tracking
var qitchBuffer = Buffer.read
(Server.default,"/Users/marinos/Library/Application Support/
SuperCollider/Extensions/SC3plugins/PitchDetection/extraqitchfiles/
QspeckernN2048SR44100.wav"); // path to auxiliary wav file for Qitch
{ // a complex signal
  var sound = Saw.ar(LFNoise2.ar(1).range(500,1000).poll(label:
\ActualFrequency)) + WhiteNoise.ar(0.4);
  ZeroCrossing.ar(sound).poll(label:\ZeroCross);
  Pitch.kr(sound).poll(label:\Pitch);
  Tartini.kr(sound).poll(label:\Tartini);
  Qitch.kr(sound,qitchBuffer).poll(label:\Qitch);
  Out.ar(0,sound!2);
}.play;
)
```

For this signal, Qitch is probably the most reasonable choice, judging by the output on my machine:

```
ActualFrequency: 864.222
ZeroCross: 6368.27
Pitch: 171.704
Pitch: 1
Tartini: 95.0917
Tartini: 1
Qitch: 845.466
Qitch: 1
```

Timbre analysis and feature detection

Timbre is a psycho-acoustic quality, and refers to what makes sounds distinct even if they have the same loudness and pitch. Of course this is a broad oversimplification of a very complex subject; in reality there isn't even a consensus on what exactly timbre stands for. While timbre has been proposed to depend on several qualities, in a machine listening context timbre recognition is almost exclusively based on analyzing spectra. Herein, we will focus on how to broadly detect several spectral features, rather than timbre per se, which is a rather indefinite quality. By the term feature we refer to anything that could be characteristic about a signal's spectral characteristics.

In SuperCollider there is a plethora of relevant UGens, both in the standard distribution as well as in extension libraries. Of the most useful are `SpecCentroid` and `ScpeFlatness` used to calculate the **spectral centroid** and the **spectral flatness**, respectively. The former roughly stands for the most perceptually prominent frequency range in our signal while the latter is an indicator of how complicated our signal is (for example, for a sinusoid it would be 0 while for white noise close to 1). The `SpecPcile` UGen will calculate the cumulative distribution of a spectrum, and given a percentile of spectral energy as an argument, will return that frequency from which the given percentile of spectral energy lies below. In the SC3Plugins extensions bundle we will also find the `FFTCrest` UGen, which will calculate the **spectral crest** of a signal, which, in short, indicates how flat or peaky a signal is, and the `SensoryDissonance` UGen, which will attempt to calculate how dissonant a signal is (with 1 being totally dissonant and 0 being totally consonant). The `FFTSpread` UGen measures the **spectral spread** of a signal, that is how wide or narrow its spectrum is and `FFTSlope` calculates the slope of the linear correlation line derived from the spectral magnitudes. Finally, the `Goertzel` UGen calculates the magnitude and phase at a single specified frequency. For example:

```
( // feature extraction
{  var sound = SinOsc.ar(240,mul:0.5)
  + Resonz.ar(ClipNoise.ar,2000,0.6,mul:SinOsc.kr(0.05).range(0,0.5))
  + Saw.ar(2000,mul:SinOsc.kr(0.1).range(0,0.3));
  var fft = FFT(LocalBuf(2048),sound);  // a complex signal
  SpecCentroid.kr(fft).poll(label:\Centroid);
  SpecFlatness.kr(fft).poll(label:\Flatness);
  SpecPcile.kr(fft,0.8).poll(label:\Percentile);
  FFTCrest.kr(fft,1800,2200).poll(label:\Crest);
  SensoryDissonance.kr(fft).poll(label:\Dissonance);
  Out.ar(0,sound!2);
}.play;
)
```

Onset detection and rhythmical analysis

There are some specialized UGens we can use to perform beat tracking, which is to analyze the rhythmical characteristics of a signal. BeatTrack, for example, will return an array comprising of the current detected tempo as well as impulse ticks at quarter, eighth, and sixteenth note ratios. Note that it takes about six seconds for it to start predicting. A similar in spirit beat tracker is BeatTrack2, which, however, follows a different approach internally. An example with BeatTrack is as follows:

```
( // Beatracking example
var buffer = Buffer.read(Server.default, "/path/to/some/audio/file/
with/prominent/rhythm");
 // use an audio file with prominent rhythm here
{   var sound = PlayBuf.ar(1,buffer,BufRateScale.ir(buffer),loop:1)*4;
.// loop through the file
  var fft = FFT(LocalBuf(512),sound);
  var analysis = BeatTrack.kr(fft); // analyze it
  var tempo = analysis[3].poll(label:\EstimatedTempo);
.// print the estimated tempo
  var beat = Decay.kr(analysis[1],0.2) * WhiteNoise.ar(0.1);
 // clicks produced on the  right channel
  Out.ar(0,[sound,beat]);
}.play;
)
```

Supercollider also features a series of UGens which we can use to perform the **onset detection**. Onset detectors, generally speaking, have the ability to spot changes. Depending on both—the kind of signal and the algorithm we use—these changes may signify tonal, chord, morphological, spectral, or other kinds of permutations. The most important time-domain onset detectors are the Coyote (to be found in the SC3Plugins extensions bundle) and Slope UGens, the first of which performs a sophisticated amplitude analysis and the latter measures the rate of a signal's change per second. Slope will return an array of two instances of OutProxy. Several specialized onset detectors are available too, for example, PV_HainsworthFoote, PV_JensenAndersen, and Onsets UGens, the latter specializing in musical signals. We can see all of them in action in the following example; note that some of those UGens outputs trigger, which won't be visible if polled directly, therefore we have them trigger a nominal signal instead.

```
( // onset detection example
Server.default.waitForBoot({
   {   // a complex signal
     var sound, sequence, fft, analysis;
     sequence = Demand.kr(Impulse.kr(2),0,
Dseq([[250,300],[420,650],[100,150],[1000,2300]],inf));
     sound = Saw.ar(sequence,mul:0.2)+
Resonz.ar(ClipNoise.ar(),sequence,0.3,1);
```

```
    sound = sound * EnvGen.ar(Env([0,1,0],[0,0.5]),Impulse.kr(2));
    Coyote.kr(sound).poll(label:\Coyote);
    Slope.ar(sound).poll(label:\Slope);
    fft = FFT(LocalBuf(512),Mix.new(sound));
    analysis = PV_HainsworthFoote.ar(fft,0.5,0.5,threshold:1);
    K2A.ar(1).poll(K2A.ar(analysis),label:\HainsworthFoote);
    analysis = PV_JensenAndersen.ar(fft,threshold:0.2);
    K2A.ar(1).poll(K2A.ar(analysis),label:\JensenAndersen);
    analysis = Onsets.kr(fft,threshold:1);
    K2A.ar(1).poll(K2A.ar(analysis),label:\Onsets);
    Out.ar(0,sound);
  }.play;
})
)
```

Basic mappings

Having discussed both how to acquire data and how to extract information out of audio signals, it is time to discuss how we can map them to other ranges so that we can use them to control visual elements, or in general, other parts of our programs. As far as mappings are concerned, we can distinguish between a series of tasks that are likely to be involved namely, *generate*, *acquire*, *store*, *probe*, *preprocess*, and finally *encode* and *distribute*. Depending on the nature of each project and of the kind of data involved, some of these steps might be non applicable or may be extrinsic to SuperCollider and in exceptional cases it could be that more steps are involved. We have already talked extensively about how to generate data by means of analyzing signals as well as about how to acquire them from various sources, and while doing so, we have also demonstrated ways in which we can store data.

Before we elaborate on the later stages, we need to briefly discuss a fundamental schism in SuperCollider's architecture namely, the one between the *Server* (that is, the audio synthesis engine(s)) and the *Client* or *SCLang* (these refer to the SuperCollider programming language). These two parts of SuperCollider are largely independent, information exchange carried out internally using the OSC protocol. We can exchange data in both directions, therefore we will have to examine both client-side and server-side mapping techniques, so that we are in a position to select the most efficient stratagem in every context. Note that while sending data from a server to the client via OSC is generally an acceptable practice, using the `poll` method as we did in the previous examples should only be used for testing purposes and never in final projects since it is a CPU-intensive task.

Preparing and preprocessing data on the client side

It is probably the norm, rather than the exception, that a dataset will require some sort of preparation before we can go on and use it. This may happen for several reasons. For example, our dataset might not be in the right format; it may contain strings or booleans when what we really need are floats. It is also very typical that data may have been corrupted resulting in invalid entries that need to be filtered out. It is also quite often the case that we need to compensate for software/hardware inaccuracies or for random environmental events that might have biased our data. For example, some machine listening algorithm which failed to identify pitch in somebody's cough, or some kind of hardware measurement device which was affected by somebody's cellphone, or by electrical induction. More importantly, it is quite often the case that the kind of information we need can only be acquired if we somehow analyze the data, for technical or other reasons. Imagine for example, that we are interested in tracking frequencies only within the range 400-800 Hz: the only way to do this is to first track frequencies and then filter out those that are outside our range of interest.

Of course there is no predefined way to prepare our data, but there are some fundamental methodologies based upon which we can achieve all kinds of complex manipulations. First thing to consider is that we need to perform **data tests** so that we know if and what kind of invalid data there may exist. Tests can be either inclusive, that is, to test if every unique entry is valid, or exclusive, that is, to test if there are invalid entries in our dataset. The former is safer but the latter may be faster, as we don't have to test every single element. Of course when a real-time dataflow is concerned, we will have to appropriate these techniques so that they are meaningful in this context. At a more rudimentary level, we will probably have to perform tests to find out in what form our data has arrived, as this is unknown sometimes. Consider, for example, this cardiac arrhythmia data that we have retrieved from the Internet in the beginning of our chapter. Let's perform some basic tests to see in what form the data has arrived:

```
// probing a dataset
~data = CSVFileReader.read("arrhythmia.data".absolutePath,true,true);
// read data
~data.class; // dataset it is an instance of Array
~data.collect(_.species).as(IdentitySet); // containing other Arrays
~data.size; // 452 of them actually
~data.flatten.collect(_.species).as(IdentitySet);
// each of which contains Strings
```

Now, having determined the structure of our dataset, we can decide what kind of transformations we will need to perform before we can actually use that data in a specific project. Indeed, we will most likely have to convert it into a monodimensional array with numbers, rather than strings.

Apparently, the kinds of tests we need to do largely depend on what we want to do subsequently with our data. In this example, we demonstrated how to use generic methods such as `size`, `species`, and `as` to perform basic tests. `collect(_.species)` is just a shortcut for `collect{arg item; item.species}`. `collect` merely evaluates the given function for each element and returns a new collection containing the results. A very useful trick is to then convert the dataset into an instance of the `IdentitySet` class, this ways removing all duplicate entries. In this particular case, we do so in order to see what kinds (`species`) of objects our dataset consists of, but in a different context we could have done so to probe the kind of different elements a dataset would consist of. More useful testing methods are inherited to all collections by their base class `Collection`, such as `includes` (tests if some object is included in the collection), `includesAny` (tests whether any of a series of objects in included), `includesAll` (tests whether all given objects are included), `occurrencesOf` (returns the number of occurrences of an object in the collection), `any` (answers whether a given instance of `Function` returns `true` for at least one item in the collection), `every` (answers whether a given instance of `Function` returns `true` for at least one item in the collection), and `count` (answers the number of items for which a given instance of `Function` returns `true`).

As far as manipulating the `Collection` base class is concerned, we can apply almost any possible transformation by using `collect`, `select`, or `reject`. The latter will evaluate the given instance of `Function` for every item and will return a new collection consisting of only those items for which it returned `true` (for select) or `false` (for reject). And of course any other method that maybe useful. To see how this works in practice, we will now assume that we are only interested in non-repeating, non-zero entries out of our arrhythmia dataset, and that we want to omit (rather than substitute) all invalid entries. We could proceed as follows:

```
// filter irrelevant data
~data = ~data.flatten.collect(_.asInteger);
// convert to mono-dimensional array of Integers
~data = ~data.select(_!=0); // remove zeros
~data = ~data.as(IdentitySet).asArray;
/* convert to IdentitySet and back to Array to filter out duplicates */
```

Preparing and preprocessing data on the server side

Thereafter, preprocessing on server side is very different in philosophy. Firstly, we will not normally need to probe our data to find out what their structure is, and what they consist of; since every kind of information handled by the server is already a signal of some sort. Indeed, the only kind of data we may acquire at server side is data retrieved by analyzing signals. Secondly, all operations that we can perform on signals are exclusively via UGens or via certain operations (which technically redirect to UGens themselves). That being said, the kind of manipulations we can do is far from fundamental, there are specialized objects for all kinds of simple and more sophisticated operations. As far as tests are concerned, there are operations or UGens that will return either 1 or 0 with respect to some input's characteristic.

To test some signal against some range of values, we may use the `InRange` UGen, or the various comparison operations (`>`, `<`, `>=`, `<=`) we had introduced in *Chapter 2, Waveform Synthesis*. We can also apply logic operations on the results using the bitwise operations we examined in the same chapter. The `Schmidt` UGen will output 1 when the input rises above a certain *high* threshold and keep on generating 1 until the input falls below a given *low* threshold, in which case it will output 0 until the input rises again above *high*, and so on. There are several ways we can exploit the results of such tests. The `if` UGen operation expects two signals as its *true* and *false* arguments, respectively, and will output the first signal if its receiver is 1 or the second signal if its receiver is 0. Note that the input has to be either 1 or 0, else it will output a mixture of both the *true* and *false* clauses, which might be ok for synthesis purposes but it may not for manipulating data. We could also use the `Gate` UGen, which will only let input values to pass if given a positive value; else it will keep sending the last value. There are other ways to control the signal flow within a UGen graph, for example, using the `Select` UGen, which will select a signal from an array given its index. In this context, we could, for instance, rely on **count UGens**, such as `PulseCount` or `Stepper` to count the number of triggers received by some machine listening UGens and have things happen when the triggers equal a certain number.

There are numerous other UGens that we may use to directly or indirectly manipulate signals within our UGen graph and achieve simple and more sophisticated data filtering; Decay, Decay2, and Integrator, will cause a trigger to last longer, so that we can use it to control other signals; TrigAvg will average the absolute values of its input between the received triggers; Limiter will limit the input values to never exceed a certain level; Lag and its other instance methods (Lag2, Lag3, LagUD, Lag2UD, Lag3UD, and VarLag) will delay the rate of change of our data; Slew will limit the slope of our input; Ramp will break continuous data flow into linear segments of specific duration; Latch will *sample and hold* input signals when triggered; Trig1 will output 1 for a specified duration when triggered; Normalizer will normalize the input amplitude to the given level. Generally speaking, it may take some thought and imagination to come up with plausible ways to implement some particular manipulation on our data, yet we can achieve very sophisticated ones by means of combining the aforementioned UGens. In the following example, we use a number of techniques to perform tests and data manipulation, our aim being to produce a noise pulse after 10 onset detections and only when the input's frequency at this point is above 800 Hz or below 300 Hz:

```
( // server-side testing & filtering
  {  var sound, fft, onset, freq, analysis;
     sound = Saw.ar(LFNoise2.kr(2).range(100,1000));
 // a complex signal
     freq = Tartini.kr(sound); // frequency tracking
     sound = sound * EnvGen.kr(Env([0,1,0],[2,1],[\cubed,\step]).
circle) * BrownNoise.ar();
 // Ring modulate with BrownNoise and apply an envelope
     fft = FFT(LocalBuf(512),Mix.new(sound));
 // fft for the onsets detector
     onset = Onsets.kr(fft,threshold:1); // detect onsets
     analysis = ( Decay.kr(onset) & ((Decay.kr(freq[1]) &
(freq[0] > 800)) | ( Decay.kr(freq[1]) & (freq[0]<200))));
 /* 1 if there is an onset AND the detected frequency is being
detected to be either above 800 or below 200 */
     analysis.if(WhiteNoise.ar(),Silent.ar()) + (sound * 0.7);
 // mix signal with a noise pulse if the above is true
  }.play;
)
```

Basic encodings and interpolation schemes

Having prepared our data, we are ready to proceed with encoding them. In this context we have already encountered the `range` method in several examples, hitherto, to perform very basic server-side encodings. In principle, `range` assumes that the input is within the standard output range for UGens (±1) and performs the necessary math to scale any value from the input to a desired output range. In the case of `LFNoise2.ar(1).range(200,300)`, for instance, we know that for an input of `-1`, or less than `-1`, the output has to be `200`, and that for an input of `1`, or greater than `1`, the output has to be `300`. However, from a strictly mathematical perspective, knowing how to map the upper and lower bounds of a range to another is not enough, we also need a formula that will map all the in-between values accordingly. In other words, we need an **interpolation** scheme. Interpolation is a mathematical term and stands for the method to create a set of new values with respect to a discrete set of given ones.

It is important to understand that to properly (in any sense) encode a range of values to another, we need to be explicit on how data is distributed in the original range and how we want them distributed in the output one. Take for example, the output of `Pitch.kr(SinOsc.ar(LFNoise0.kr(1).range(100,1000)))`. We may consider these values as being linearly distributed since any frequency between 100 and 1000 has equal chances of being the next one at every modulation cycle. However, frequency is perceived exponentially rather than linearly, since we perceive pitch relationships as ratios: for example, two sound waves having frequencies of 100 and 200 and two others having frequencies of 500 and 1000 will be perceived by humans as having exactly the same relationship, that is, being an octave interval, even if in the first case the linear difference is 100 and in the second 500. In other words, the same numerical change signifies something different depending on the range of values we are dealing with. Now imagine that we need to map this range accordingly to control the position of some visual element in space. The latter is linearly perceived, yet we want the position of the visual element to reflect the perceived pitch rather than frequency, therefore we need an interpolation scheme that will map linearly distributed data (output of `Pitch`) with an exponential interpolation scheme, so that the smaller changes in the lower frequency range have a bigger impact than the respective in the upper, much like the way we hear.

The `range` method assumes a linear interpolation for both the input and output values and encodes data accordingly, and while this is ok for linear-to-linear mappings, we need more for other situations. Luckily there are ways to achieve other kinds of interpolation for both input and output. The `Exprange` UGen, for instance, will map linearly distributed data exponentially, as will the `curverange` method, which also allows us to modulate the exponent factor of the distribution, thus allowing us to control the curvature of the distribution. For both server-side and client-side mappings, there is a series of relating methods we can use on UGens, UGen graphs, instances of `Collection` and instances of `SimpleNumber` to achieve a wide range of possible input/output interpolation schemes as well as to control both the input and the output ranges namely `linin` (assumes linear input and output interpolation), `linexp` (linear input, exponential output; output range should not include zero), `explin` (exponential input, linear output; input range should not include zero), `expexp` (exponential input/output; both input and output ranges should not include zero), `curvelin` (custom exponential input), or `lincurve` (custom exponential output). Some examples are as follows:

```
3.linlin(-1,5,10,20);
 /* map a value if the input range is -1,5 the output 10,20 and
assuming linear input/output distributions */
[5,6,2,10,4].lincurve(-10,10,0,1,-8);
 /* map all elements of an array in the -5,10 input range to an 0,1
exponential output range */
{SinOsc.ar(SinOsc.ar(1).lincurve(-1,1,100,500,8))}.play
 /* map the output of a UGen to a custom range using a custom
exponential disctribution */
```

More specialized mapping methods also exist, for example, `bilin` (assumes two linear ranges and encodes them to two linear output ranges), `biexp` (the same but with exponential interpolation), `gaussCurve` (linear input, Gaussian output), `scurve` (linear input scurve output), and `ramp` (maps receiver onto a ramp starting at 0).

Another standard way of performing mappings on the client side is with the `ControlSpec` class, and using its `map` method which expects as arguments, a *minimum* value, a *maximum* value, an *interpolation scheme* (which could be either a number representing the exponent or a warp symbol such as `\exp`, `\lin`, and `\sine`), and a *step* value which will will map an input value (in the 0 to 1 range) accordingly. We can also use its `unmap` method to perform the opposite operation, that is to map a value in a *minimum-maximum* input range to a 0-1 output one. For example:

```
ControlSpec(100,1000,\exp,5).map(0.5);
 /* map a 0-1 linear input range to a 100,1000 output one with
exponential interpolation and at intervals of 5 */
ControlSpec(100,1000,\exp,5).unmap(315);
 /* map a 100-1000 exponential input range to a 0,1 output one with
linear interpolation and at intervals of 5 */
```

Sharing and distributing data

Equally important with manipulating and encoding data is to be able to exchange them between the different parts of our programs. There are four basic scenarios: client-side sharing between different client-side subprograms, server-side sharing between the different instances of Synth, sending data from the client to the server and vice versa. On the client, sharing data is as simple as keeping them to some (global) variable accessible to all involved subprograms. Communication between different instances of Synth in the same server can be easily achieved too, using instances of Bus or Buffer; some instance of Synth may write to a Bus or to a Buffer object and another may read data when needed. Note, however, there is no direct way to exchange data between instances of Synth running on different instances of Server, so in such cases we would have to use the client as a mediator.

Sending data from the client to the server can be achieved simply through the set or setn methods of the Synth class. Using the Control UGen we may extend their functionality to be able to also send instances of Array as arguments. For example:

```
( // Using Control UGen
Server.default.waitForBoot({fork{
    varsynth;

    SynthDef(\controlExample, { //define SynthDef
      var frequencies = Control.names([\freqs]).kr([100,200,300,400]);
      var sound = Mix.new(SinOsc.ar(frequencies)*0.1);
      Out.ar(0,sound!2);
    }).add;
    Server.default.sync; // sync with Server

    synth = Synth(\controlExample); // start synth

    fork{ loop { // modulate freqs with a loop
        var newFreqs = Array.fill(4,{arg i; rrand(100,1000)});
 // array has to be of the same size as the original
       synth.set(\freqs, newFreqs);
      1.wait;
    }};
}});
)
```

Note that we can only send instances of `Array` having the same size as the one used inside the definition of `SynhDef`. There are also several ways in which we can send data from an instance of `Server` to the client. We could, for example, use instances of `Buffer` or `Bus` and afterwards acquire data from the language using the `get` or `getn` methods, as we did in *Chapter 1*, *Scoping, Plotting, and Metering*, `LevelIndicator` example. Another approach would be to use `SendTrig` or `SendRepyUGens`, to send OSC messages to the client, and therefore, have specific tasks triggered by a `Server`. An example with `SendReply` is as follows:

```
( // Sending OSC from the Server to the Client
{    var freqs  = LFNoise0.kr([1,1]).exprange(100,500);
  SendReply.kr(Impulse.kr(1),'/freq',freqs,replyID:1);
 /* send a message with the current freqs when a trigger is received */
  SinOsc.ar(freqs); // output sound
}.play;
OSCFunc({ arg msg;
  msg.postln; // print the message to the post window
}, '/freq',Server.default.addr);
 /* respond only to message /freq coming from the default Server's
address */.
 )
```

Notice that the OSC message received is an array containing the OSC path, the node ID of the sender's instance of `Synth` and the `replyID` parameter that we have set, along with the actual data sent. Therefore, we may easily distinguish which instance of `Synth` sent the message if we have more than one.

A special case of data sharing is when we want to share data created by some **pattern** within some `Pbind` or `Pmono` structure. The easiest way to deal with such cases is to use the `collect` method. The currently playing `Event object` will be passed implicitly to the latter as an argument, which we may copy to a variable and use at will, as in the following example:

```
( // sending data retrieved from Patterns
Server.default.waitForBoot({fork{
  var data; // we will store the currently playing event here
  SynthDef(\mySound, { arg freqA,freqB;
    var signal;
    signal = SinOsc.ar([freqA,freqB]);
    Out.ar(0,signal*0.5);
  }).add; // add synthDef
  Server.default.sync; // and sync with Server
```

```
Pmono(\mySound,  // a Pmono
  \freqA, Pbrown(100,500,100,inf),
  \freqB, Pbrown(100,500,100,inf)
).collect({ arg event;
  data = event; // here we pass the current even to data
}).play;

1.wait; // wait a second so that data is given some value

fork{loop{ // do something with the data
  [data.freqA, data.freqB].postln;
  1.wait;
}}
}});
)
```

Summary

In this chapter, we discussed efficient ways to acquire, probe, preprocess, manipulate, encode, and exchange data within our programs. We also touched upon various communication protocols and ways in which we can retrieve data from remote clients as well as from specialized hardware, and also discussed machine listening techniques and ways to retrieve information from audio signals.

In the next chapter, we will see how we can combine such techniques with vector graphics and animation methodologies, to implement complex data, audio, and music visualizers.

7
Advanced Visualizers

Having discussed vector graphics, animation, machine listening as well as several techniques to manipulate and encode data, we are now ready to start implementing more advanced visualizers. In this chapter, we will demonstrate how to practically deal with a wide range of visualization scenarios through a series of examples based on the miscellaneous structures and techniques that we have already discussed in the previous chapters. Even if we are primarily interested in visualization here, we will implicitly discuss sonification as well, the latter sometimes being intrinsic and indispensable to the former.

The topics that will be covered in this chapter are as follows:

- Complex waveform visualizers
- Spectrogram
- Visualizing patterns
- Visualizing with sprites and kinematic structure
- Visualizers based on particle systems and fractals
- Sonifying numerical data

Audio visualizers

Having elaborated on more complex graphics and animation techniques, it does make sense to briefly revisit the fundamentals of audio scoping and examine how we can further exploit the built-in visualizers as well as how to implement our own, more advanced ones.

Trailing waveforms

Regarding how to further exploit existent visualizers, we could, for instance, layer the distinct semi-transparent instances of the `ScopeView` class and modulate their horizontal zoom factors periodically and at different rates to achieve accelerated trailing effects.

For example:

```
var window = /* create parent window here */

var buffers= Array.fill(8,{Buffer.alloc(Server.default,1024,2)});
 // an Array of 8 buffers

var scopes = Array.fill(8,{arg i;
   ScopeView(window,Rect(0,0,640,480))
  .bufnum_(buffers[i].bufnum) // associate with the right Buffer
  .backColor_(Color(0.6,0.8,0.9,1/4)) // notice the alpha channel
  .waveColors_([Color.green,Color.yellow]);
});

/* modulate horizontal zoom factor on all views with respect to their
index */
fork{loop{
  scopes.do{arg item,index;
    {item.xZoom_( 4 + (3*(sin((Main.elapsedTime / 2) +
    (index*0.02)))))));}.defer;
  };
  0.1.wait; // change factor every 0.1 seconds
}};

// now synthesize something and write it to the Buffers
// ...
```

There is not much to comment here as the code is simple and straightforward. The idea is to conceptually treat the instances of the `ScopeView` class as ordinary visual elements and rely on standard animation techniques to make their appearance more interesting. Albeit in this case implementation is trivial, the underlying idea is not an easy one for someone without any experience in computer graphics.

The full code for this example can be found online in this book's code bundle using two of the waveforms that we synthesized in *Chapter 2, Waveform Synthesis*. The result would look as follows:

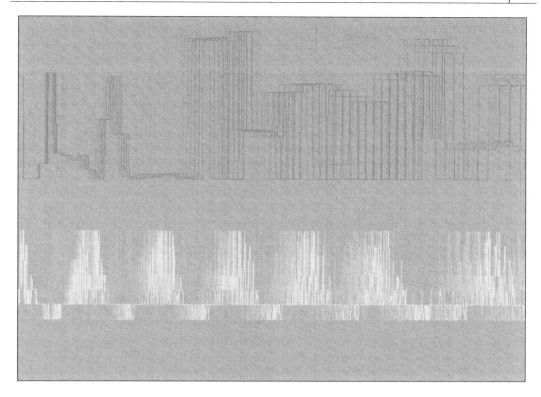

Spectrogram

We have already demonstrated how to achieve frequency scoping using the SuperCollider's built-in `FreqScopeView` class. Nevertheless, SuperCollider lacks a built-in **spectrogram**. Spectrograms represent how spectra evolves over time, typically by means of mapping time in the horizontal axis, frequency on the vertical axis, and amplitude using different shades of gray or some other color code. Since it is pretty useful and nice to have such a tool around, we will implement a custom spectrogram class herein. In our implementation, we directly access the spectral data (that we analyze using `FFT` and save to a `Buffer` class beforehand), and after processing it accordingly, we map its intensities to shades of grey using `Image`. For reasons of efficiency and to avoid performing unnecessary calculations, we use an array of instances of the `Image` class, each of which represents a single column that is 1pixel in width. Then, starting with an array of empty columns, we `rotate` it at every subsequent frame (so that all the columns move one position to the left and the first becomes the last), and update the pixel values of the last column alone according to the spectral data that is currently available. This will result in spectra moving at a uniform speed towards the left, the current spectrum being the outer right.

Our `drawFunc` will then look as follows:

```
.drawFunc_({
  this.updateColumns.value;
 // call this instance's updateColumns' method
  // draw columns once next to each other starting from the left
  mColumns.do{ arg image,index;
    image.drawAtPoint(Point(index,0),image.bounds);
  };
});
```

Analyzing and storing the spectral data to a buffer is trivial; all that we need is `FFT`:

```
SynthDef(\myFancySpectrogramSynth, { arg in, buf;
  FFT(buf,In.ar(Mix.new(in)));
 // just analyze audio and fill the buffer with spectral data
}).add;
```

Then from within `updateColumns`, we can directly access buffer with the spectral data and perform all calculations to update our array of images:

```
updateColumns {
 /* this methods reads/processes spectral data and updates
columns accordingly */
// read spectral data from the FFT buffer
mBuffer.getn(0, 1024,{ arg buf;
  var magnitudes, complex, data;
  { // defer
    magnitudes = buf.clump(2).flop;
 /* re-arrange spectral data so that we have a pair of
magnitudes/phases */
    complex = ((((Complex(
      Signal.newFrom( magnitudes[0] ),
      Signal.newFrom( magnitudes[1] )
    ).magnitude.reverse)).log10)*80).clip(0, 255);
 /* process spectral data accordingly so that we end up with an array
of values representing the intensity of the 512 bins as numbers in the
0-255 range */

    // convert bin intensity to pixels
    data = complex.floor.collect({arg item;
      var pixel, color;
      color = Color.grey( (255 - item) / 255 );
/* first invert bin intensity so that full intensity is black, rather
than white */
      Image.colorToPixel( color );
 /* convert color to pixel (setPixels cannot handle colors directly) */
    });
```

```
    data = data.as(Int32Array);
  /* make an Int32Array out of our bins (this is what setPixels
expects) */
    mColumns = mColumns.rotate(-1);
  /* rotate mColumns so that the first element is now the last and all
the rest are moved to the left */
    mColumns[639].setPixels(data,Rect(0,0,1,512));
  /* fill the last column with newly acquired data */
  }.defer;
});
}
```

The 1024 entries of the FFT buffer represent each bin's real part followed by its imaginary part and then the next bin's real part followed by its imaginary part, and so on. However, to set the pixels of an instance of the Image class to some specific color, we need an appropriately sized instance of the Int32Array class with color values in the internal format of Image. Hence, the only complexity with the code is to convert from one form of representation to another. To achieve this, we first convert the complex spectral data to bins' intensities in the 0-255 range, then invert these numbers so that the highest intensity corresponds to black rather than white, and finally use Image.colorToPixel to convert these ranges to the appropriate pixel number (these are internally handled by Image).

The full code can be found online in this book's code bundle. The final class also features the start and stop methods so that we can pause and resume the spectral animation at will. Once the class is compiled, we can test it as follows:

```
( // testing our myFancySpectrogram
Server.default.waitForBoot({ fork { // boot server and start a routine
  var spectrogram;
    {spectrogram = MyFancySpectrogram.new(0)}.defer;
  // a new spectrogram
    1.wait; // wait a bit before starting scoping;
    {spectrogram.start}.defer; // start scoping
    // an audio signal to test
    {   Resonz.ar(ClipNoise.ar,15000,0.01,mul:SinOsc.kr(0.2)
      .range(0,1))
      + Saw.ar(LFTri.kr(0.1).range(200,5060),mul:0.2)
      + ( Klang.ar('[[800, 803, 8011],[0.3, 0.7, 0.4],[0, 0, pi]])
        * SinOsc.kr(0.5).range(0,2) );
    }.play;
  };
});
)
```

The result is illustrated in the following screenshot:

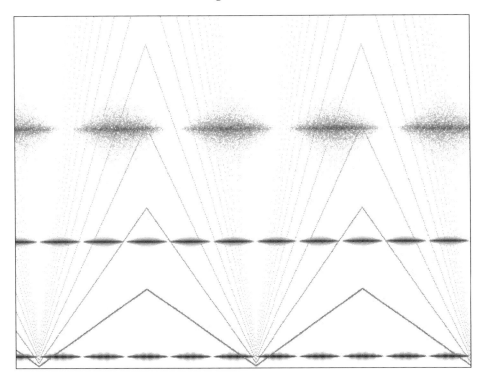

Note that this implementation maps the frequencies linearly. Coding a logarithmic version is left as an exercise to the reader. Also note that since the Image class is broken in the current (at the time of writing this) stable version of SuperCollider, we will have to use a more recent build (3.7 or greater) for this code to work properly.

 It is a common practice in object oriented programming to prefix all the instance variables inside a class with the letter m, so that we can easily distinguish them from the local ones.

Music visualizers

In this section, we will attempt more imaginative visualizers wherein our visual structures will be animated not according to some signal's waveform or spectral characteristics, but rather with respect to more abstract musical properties such as the frequency of a particular element or the output of some pattern.

Rotating windmills

In this example, we rotate five windmills with respect to the detected frequencies of five complex sound sources. Each of our five instances of Synth also writes the frequency information (tracked in real time via Tartini) to an instance of Bus to be accessed later by our drawFunc function and set the rotational speed accordingly. Herein, we rely on the windmill factory we had demonstrated in *Chapter 5, Animation* (which, of course, we have to load again). We will then create five instances of Synth using the following instance of SynthDef:

```
SynthDef(\windmillVisualizerSynth, { arg freqOut, rate;
  var signal, modulator, analysis;
  modulator = LFNoise2.ar(rate).range(100,1000);
  signal = Saw.ar(modulator) * 0.2;
  analysis = Tartini.kr(signal); // analyze signal
  signal = signal!2; // mix signal and make stereo
  Out.kr(freqOut, analysis[0]); // output to a control bus
  Out.ar(0,signal);
}).add; // add synthDef
```

We will use the freqOut argument to write the output of those instances of Synth to an array of five Buses, and once we have created five instances of our windmill object too, we can simply rotate them with respect to the frequencies of each instance of Synth inside our drawFunc function, as shown in the following code:

```
windmills.do{arg item, index; // for each windmill
  // calculate speed from frequency
  var speed = buses[index].getSynchronous.explin(100,1000,20,10);
 // encode frequency to speed factor
  Pen.push;
  Pen.rotate((userView.frame/speed).cos,
item.position.x,item.position.y);
  // divide frame count with speed factor
  item.draw();
  Pen.pop;
}
```

The full code for this example can be found online in this book's code bundle. A still from the animation is illustrated in the following screenshot:

Kinematic patterns

In the following example, we will exemplify how we can exchange data between patterns in a running event player and our visualizer. Pwalk is a pattern emulating a one-dimensional random walk over the values in its argument list. Herein we use two instances of the Pwalk class to simulate a kinematic snake's wandering in a two-dimensional space, apparently using the snake factory, as we had discussed in *Chapter 5, Animation*. The very data used as the frequency coefficients of our sound generator will be used to control our snake's positioning in the canvas, therefore visualizing the random walk and also accentuating the particular nature of our sound synthesis algorithm.

Since we rely on the snake factory that we had introduced in *Chapter 5, Animation*, we will have to load it again here:

```
(PathName(thisProcess.nowExecutingPath).pathOnly ++
"/9677OS_07_snake_factory.scd").loadPaths;
 // first load the windmill factory
```

We will use the following instance of the SynthDef class as a sound source:

```
SynthDef(\mySound, { arg freqA, freqB;
  var signal = SinOsc.ar([freqA*0.9, freqA*1.1]);
  signal = signal + BrownNoise.ar(0.3);
  signal = signal * SinOsc.ar(freqB).range(0,1);
  signal = LPF.ar(signal,400);
  Out.ar(0,signal*0.5);
}).add; // add SynthDef
```

And then we can rely on a Pmono structure to play it back, and using collect, as we had demonstrated in the previous chapter, we can access data from the currently playing instance of the Event class and store them into some variable as follows:

```
tempo = TempoClock.new(10); // new TempoClock
sound = Pmono(\mySound,
  \freqA, Pwalk((100..800),Pbrown(-5,5,1,inf).trunc,1,200.rand),
  \freqB, Pwalk((100..800),Pbrown(-5,5,1,inf).trunc,1,200.rand)
).collect({ arg event;
  data = event; // assign currently playing event to data
}).play(tempo,quant:Quant(quant: 1, timingOffset: 0.1));
```

Then we can easily update the snake's positioning with respect to our patterns as follows:

```
.drawFunc_({
  var newPosition = Point(
    data.freqA.explin(100,800,1,640),
    data.freqB.explin(100,800,1,480)
  );
  snake.refresh(newPosition); // update snake's position
  snake.draw();  // draw snake
});
```

The full code for this example is also available online in this book's code bundle.

A still from the previous example's visualization is as follows:

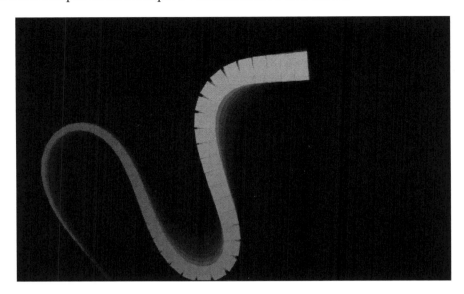

 A **random walk** is a mathematical formalization that refers to a path consisting of a succession of random steps.

Visualizing and sonifying data

Numerical data is essentially arbitrary, having no explicit signification on its own unless we somehow contextualize them. For instance, consider the cardiac arrhythmia data that we downloaded in the previous chapter; we know that they are related to somebody's heart because we were told so; else there would be no way to tell for ourselves merely by probing them. By means of visualizing or sonifying data, we are explicitly controlling the specifics of its (re) contextualization, and hence, we need to be aware that it is largely upon our particular stratagem that data is granted meaningful. In this section, we will demonstrate how we can implement data-driven audiovisual systems.

Particles and grains

In the following example, we combine a particle system with a granular synthesis engine to reanimate these arrhythmia measurements. Each piece of data is associated with a visual particle and a sonic grain. At any given time, we spawn as many particles as needed to populate the whole canvas and create the same number of sonic grains. In our example, we control after how many frames we will retrieve the subsequent pieces of data so that the resulting visualization/sonification may be constantly updated and dynamically linked to our dataset in a way that we can still control the speed of the data flow.

We first need to retrieve and preprocess the arrhythmia data. Assuming that they are still kept in a file within our home folder, we can proceed as follows:

```
// retrieve data
data = CSVFileReader.read("arrhythmia.data".absolutePath,true,true);
// preprocess data
data = data.flatten.collect(_.asInteger);
 // convert to mono-dimensional array of Integers
data = data.select(_!=0); // remove zeros
data = data.collect(_.abs); // make all positive
dataMax = data.max; // store maximum value
dataMin = data.min; // store minimum value
data = data.reshape((data.size/4).asInteger,4);
 /* convert to a 2D Array containing 4-entried datasets - first will
be radius, the rest 3 color */
```

In the following example, we will use three sinusoids per grain:

```
SynthDef(\grain, { arg freqA, freqB, freqC, duration;
  var sound;
  sound = [ SinOsc.ar(freqA),SinOsc.ar(freqB)];
  sound = sound + Pan2.ar(SinOsc.ar(freqC),0);
  sound = sound * EnvGen.ar(Env.sine(duration),doneAction:2);
  sound = sound * duration * 0.2;
  Out.ar(0,sound)
}).add; // add synthDef
```

Therefore, we need to encode the data according to the radius and color (for each particle), three frequency coefficients, and duration (for every associated grain):

```
data = data.collect{arg item;
  var radius, color, freq, duration;
  radius = item[0].curvelin(dataMin,dataMax,0,40,-6);
 // encode radiuses to be 0-60
  color = Color.new255(
    red:item[1].explin(dataMin,dataMax,0,255),
    green:item[2].explin(dataMin,dataMax,0,255),
    blue:item[3].explin(dataMin,dataMax,0,255)
  );
  freq = [
    item[1].expexp(dataMin,dataMax,200,4000),
    item[2].expexp(dataMin,dataMax,200,4000),
    item[3].expexp(dataMin,dataMax,200,4000),
  ];
  duration = item[0].explin(dataMin,dataMax,0,0.2);
  [radius, color, freq, duration];
}; /* at this point every element of data is a [radius, color, freq,
duration] array */
```

We opted to filter out all the zeros in the preprocess stage since there was an abundance of zeros in the original dataset; we could leave them in as well, but we would have to use some other encoding scheme more appropriate to the new distribution.

We can spawn grains and particles according to the encoded data using a function (that we will invoke from within `drawFunc`) as follows:

```
engine = { arg width, height, distance, dataset, index;
  (width/distance).floor.do{arg ix; // loop over the horizontal axis
    (height/distance).floor.do{arg iy; // loop over the vertical axis
      var x,y;
      var color, radius, xoffset, yoffset;
      color = dataset.wrapAt(index+ix+iy)[1];
 // wrapAt so that it loops
      radius = dataset.wrapAt(index+ix+iy)[0];
 // wrapAt so that it loops
      x = (distance/2) + (ix * distance); // calculate coordinates
      y = (distance/2) + (iy * distance); // calculate coordinates
      Pen.fillColor_(color); // set color
      Pen.addArc(x@y,radius,0,2pi); // draw a circle
      Pen.fill; // fill it
      Synth(\grain,[ // generate a grain per particle
        \freqA, dataset.wrapAt(index+ix+iy)[2][0],
        \freqB, dataset.wrapAt(index+ix+iy)[2][1],
        \freqC, dataset.wrapAt(index+ix+iy)[2][2],
        \duration, dataset.wrapAt(index+ix+iy)[3]
      ])}}};
```

The engine function features a double-nested loop that iterates through both the horizontal and the vertical dimensions to create particles at equal distances from each other. Now all that we need to do is invoke it from within our drawFunc function with the right arguments; those are the dimensions of UserView, the distance between the centers of adjacent particles, the dataset, and an index that indicates a position offset within our dataset. By incrementing an index, we proceed forward to visualizing subsequent portions of the data; therefore, the slower the index increments, the slower the visualization rate and vice versa.

For example:

```
.drawFunc_({
    if (( userView.frame % 2) == 0) {index = index + 1};
  // increment index every two frames
    engine.(640,640, 70, data, index);  // run engine
});
```

The full code can be found online in this book's code bundle. The following image is a still from the visualization:

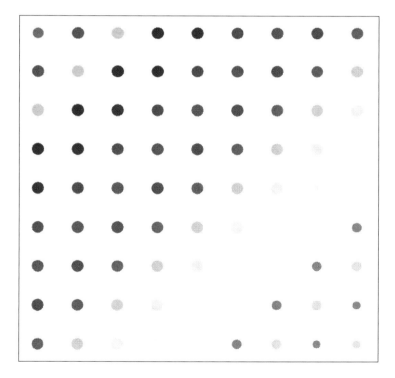

Fractalizer

In this final example, we will illustrate how we can create a data-driven fractal. The idea is to retrieve a set of points, create a shape out of them, and have it repeated over an arbitrary number of levels and branches. For our shape to be more interesting, we will also scale between subsequent levels to achieve a spiral-like fractal.

A possible factory is given herein:

```
( // a spiral fractal factory
~spiralFractalFactory = { arg numLevels, numBranches, points, colors =
[Color.red, Color.green];

  var fChildren, fractal;
  var fractalFunc = thisFunction;
// assign thisFunction to a variable

  // generate children fractals
  if (numLevels > 0) { // if there are more levels to go
    var childrenPoints, childrenRadius;

    // calculate the children positions for each for the branches
    childrenPoints = points!numBranches; // points are the same

    /* for each level generate all branches and add them to fChildren
array */
    numBranches.do{ arg i;
      fChildren = fChildren.add(fractalFunc.(numLevels-1, numBranches,
      childrenPoints[i],colors));
    };
  } { // else set children to nil
    fChildren = nil;
  };

  // create fractal object
  fractal = (
    children: fChildren,
/* an array with the children (all of them fractal objects, too), or
nil */
    branches: numBranches,    // how many branches
    originalPoints: points,
    counter: 0,
    animatePoints: nil, // to be updated by animate
    colors: colors,
    animate: { arg self, speed = 0.01, centerPoint;
      var localCounter;
      self.counter = self.counter + speed; // increment counter
      localCounter = self.counter.fold2(1).abs;
```

```
    // set animate points
    self.animatePoints = Array.fill(self.branches, { arg i;
      self.originalPoints * (localCounter.sin);
    });

    Pen.scale(0.99,0.99); // scale the whole fractal

    self.branches.do{arg i; // for each branch
      Pen.moveTo(self.animatePoints[i][0]); // start at first point
      Pen.scale(0.99,0.99); // scale subsequent segments
      Pen.rotate(i/2pi, centerPoint.x,centerPoint.y);
// rotate subsequent segments
      Pen.strokeColor_(colors[0].blend(colors[1],localCounter));
// gradually move to target color

      // create segments to all subsequent points
      self.animatePoints[i].do { arg point;
        Pen.lineTo(point);
      };

      Pen.stroke; // draw strokes only
    };

    // animate children
    if (self.children.notNil) { // if there are children
      // draw all of their branches
      self.children.do{arg item;
        item.animate(speed,centerPoint);
      };
    };
  };
);

  fractal; // explicitly return fractal
};
)
```

In our following example, we will use an instance of `Routine` to create new fractal objects using our factory and with respect to random data retrieved in real time by `http://random.org`. We will ask for different sets of data so that we determine the `points` and `colors` variables of every fractal independently. The same data used for determining the `points` variable will be also encoded accordingly to create glissando trajectories in the audio part. We will repeat this process every 15 seconds so that we constantly get new fractals.

Our instance of Routine part would appear as follows:

```
// retrieve and encode data
  loop = fork{loop{ { // defer
    var data, points, colors;

    // retrieve points
    "curl \"http://www.random.org/integers/?num=10&min=1&max=640&col=1
&base=10&format=plain&rnd=new\"  > data.temp".unixCmd({
 // this function is called when the process has exited
      data = FileReader.read("data.temp", delimiter: '\n');
      data = data.collect(_.asInteger); // convert to Integer
      data = data.reshape(6,2); // reshape as pairs
      points = data.collect(_.asPoint); // convert to Point
      "rm data.temp".unixCmd; // delete temporary file

      // map points as frequencies for our Synths
      points.do{ arg point;
        var freqA, freqB;
        freqA = point.x.linlin(0,640,100,1000); // linear mapping
        freqB = point.y.linlin(0,640,100,1000); // linear mapping
        sound.free; // first stop previous synth
        sound = Synth(\gliss,[\freqA, freqA,\freqB, freqB, \dur, 15]);
      };

      // retrieve colors
      "curl \"http://www.random.org/integers/?num=6&min=1&max=255&col=
1&base=10&format=plain&rnd=new\"  > data.temp".unixCmd({
 // this function is called when the process has exited
      data = FileReader.read("data.temp", delimiter: '\n');
      data = data.collect(_.asInteger); // convert to Integer
      data = data.reshape(2,3);  // reshape as triples
      colors = [
        Color.new255(data[0][0],data[0][1],data[0][2]),
        Color.new255(data[1][0],data[1][1],data[1][2]),
      ];
      "rm data.temp".unixCmd; // delete temporary file
    });

    // create a new fractal
    fractal = ~spiralFractalFactory.value(4,3,points,colors);
  });
  }.defer;
    15.wait; // repeat process every 15 seconds
  }};
```

And then we simply invoke our new `fractal` object's `animate` from within `drawFunc`. Note that if we access `www.random.org` synchronously, our program would freeze until all data has been retrieved. This would cause glitches in both our animation and sound synthesis. This is why we use the asynchronous `unixCmd` method herein to retrieve the data. We ask the shell to download the data and save it to some temporary file. Once the command is executed, the provided instance of `Function` will be evaluated, wherein we read the data from the temporary file into the `data` variable, preprocess and encode them accordingly, and then we delete the temporary file when it's done.

The full code for the previous example can be found online in the book's code bundle. A still from the following fractal animation is shown in the following screenshot:

Summary

In this chapter, we have demonstrated how to implement advanced visualizers by means of combining several techniques and methodologies that we had previously introduced in this book. The examples cover a wide range of scenarios including how to achieve more complex waveform scoping, how to implement a spectrogram, how to visualize patterns, and musical information using sprites and kinematics structures, as well as how to implement data-driven fractals and particle systems.

In the next chapter, we will deal with more advanced topics such as automata and complex encodings and introduce ourselves to probability distributions, textual parsing, and neural networks, among others.

8
Intelligent Encodings and Automata

This chapter aspires to introduce and familiarize the reader with more advanced concepts, such as statistical data analyses, textual parsing, and ways to implement intelligent encodings. We will, further, examine the concept of automaton and demonstrate how we can implement autonomous systems that generate audiovisual structures on their own. Yet, it has to be emphasized that this chapter serves primarily as a pragmatic introduction rather than a formal treatise to the aforementioned. Even though I have done my best to ensure that the examples so far are indicative of both the complexities as well as the potential of the topics discussed, those interested in an in-depth discussion of the technical challenges involved in any of those areas should refer to more specialized resources.

The topics that will be covered in this chapter are as follows:

- Statistical analysis and probability distributions
- Textual parsing
- Intelligent encodings
- Neural networks
- Cellular automata
- The Game of Life

Analyzing data

In *Chapter 6, Data Acquisition and Mapping*, we discussed how to acquire data as well as how to generate them by means of machine-listening techniques. It is also often the case that we need to analyze non-audio signals or data collections of some sort. However, data analysis stands for an infinite range of operations we may perform on some collection; additionally, it is often the case that we blindly probe the collection for potentially interesting patterns rather than looking for something in particular. Dealing with such cases in real-life projects would be overwhelming if there were no generalized methodologies that serve as the starting point.

Fortunately, there is already a kind of science dedicated to the systemic study of the collection, organization, analysis, interpretation, and presentation of any kind of data, namely statistics. As such, it provides us with a very sophisticated background to perform analyses and feature extraction of various sorts. By applying statistical analysis to our datasets, we can easily interpret our data with respect to some desired feature (as long as we can mathematically formalize the latter) as well as probe it for interesting behavior by means of calculating some standard measures. Now we will discuss the most fundamental concepts and techniques that we can combine to achieve even more complicated analyses.

Statistical analyses and metadata

Let us introduce ourselves to some fundamental statistical notions and measures. The **mode** of data collection is the value with highest probability or, in other words, the value that appears more often. The opposite of the mode is usually referred to as the **least repeated element**. Note that, paradoxically, in a list of numbers wherein no number is repeated and all the values have equal chances of appearing, the mode is also least repeated number. The **head** of a dataset stands for those values that appear quite often, and the **tail** represents the remaining. **Mean** is the average of the data collection in question. **Median** is that value that separates the higher from the lower half of the dataset, or in other words, the "middle-value" of the dataset. **Range** is simply the distance between the lowest and the highest number. Since the later will be very misleading if our dataset includes just a couple of very big or very small numbers, an **interquartile range** (usually abbreviated as **iqr**), defined as the distance between the upper and the lower quartile, has also been introduced. **Variance** stands for the average of the squared differences of the mean. **Standard deviation** or σ (the Greek letter sigma) is the square root of the variance and, hence, another measure of dispersion. Of course, most of these measures are meaningful only for numerical data. In the following code, we will demonstrate how to calculate them for our arrhythmia dataset. Note that, apart from the standard `select` and `reject` instance methods, we also use `maxItem` and `minItem`, which will return the item that will either give the maximum or the minimum result respectively when passed to the supplied function, as shown in the following code:

```
( // calculate statistical meta-data
var data, mode, leastProbableNumber, head, tail, mean, median, range,
iqr, variance, deviation;

// first load and prepare our dataset
data =
  CSVFileReader.read("arrhythmia.data".absolutePath,true,true);
 // read from file
data = data[0].collect(_.asInteger);
// consider just a chunk and convert its elements to Integers
data = data.select(_!=0); // remove zeros

// calculate meta-data
mode = data.maxItem({arg item; data.occurrencesOf(item)});
("Mode is: " + mode).postln;
leastProbableNumber = data.minItem({arg item;
  data.occurrencesOf(item)});
("Least Probable number is: " + leastProbableNumber).postln;
head = data.select{arg item; data.occurrencesOf(item) >= 6};
// only those values that appear at least 6 times
("Head is: " + head.as(IdentitySet)).postln;
tail = data.reject{arg item; data.occurrencesOf(item) >= 6};
// values that appear less than 6 times
("Tail is: " + tail.as(IdentitySet)).postln;
mean = data.sum / data.size;
// the sum of all data divided by the size of the dataset
("Mean is: " + mean).postln;
median = data.sort[data.size/2];
// the 'middle' element when the array is sorted
("Median is: " + median).postln;
range = data.max - data.min; // range
("Range is: " + range).postln;
iqr = data.at(( (data.size/4) .. ((data.size*3)/4) ));
// return an array with only the second and the third quartilion
iqr = iqr.max - iqr.min; // calculate iqr range
("Interquartile Range is: " + iqr).postln;
variance = (data.collect{arg item; (item-
  mean).squared}).sum/data.size; // calculate variance
("Variance is: " + variance).postln;
deviation = variance.sqrt; // calculate deviation
("Deviation is: " + deviation).postln;
)
```

Calculating those measures essentially results in the generation of **metadata** (**descriptive metadata,** to be precise), which is a fundamental concept for statistics and data analysis in general.

Metadata stands for data that represents abstract characteristics, properties, or attributes of other data, which usually originate from the analysis of other data.

Probabilities and histograms

Two very important statistical notions are those of probability and of probability distribution. Probability is a measure of how likely it is for an event to happen. When dealing with discrete datasets, an event would be to retrieve the next element of a dataset. We can easily calculate probabilities by simply dividing the occurrences of a specific element within our dataset and dividing it with the latter's total size. Graphs of elements (horizontal dimension) versus their occurrences within a dataset are termed histograms and are extremely useful in allowing one to have an overview of the probability distribution of all the elements in a dataset. Naturally, nonexistent elements are represented by a probability of zero. In the following example, we will calculate probability distribution as an array of as many indices as the range of possible values in the original dataset along with entries representing how many instances of each particular index are contained in the latter. Of course, when we are dealing with negative values, we need to bias everything accordingly and then compensate for it on the graph using `Plotter` class' `domainSpecs` instance variable to set a new horizontal range. As of this writing, however, this approach will fail to properly set up the values due to an internal bug that is to be fixed in some future version of SuperCollider.

```
( // calculate a histogram
var data, histogram, histSize;
data = "curl
\"http://www.random.org/integers/?num=1000&min=-
  100&max=100&col=1&base=10&format=plain&rnd=new\"
  ".unixCmdGetStdOutLines;
 // retrieve random numbers in the range
  (-100,100) from random.org
data = data.collect(_.asInteger); // convert to integers
histSize = data.max-data.min + 1; // calculate the size
histogram = Array.fill(histSize,{0});
 // a signal with as many elements as the range of values we are
interested in
data.do({ arg item;
  var count, histoIndex;
  histoIndex = item + data.min.abs;
 // to compensate for negative items
  count = histogram.at(histoIndex); // read previous value
  histogram.put(histoIndex, count + 1); // increment it
});
histogram.plot().domainSpecs_([-100,100,\lin,1].asSpec);
 // make a histogram
 )
```

In the probability theory, independent events are those that are not affected in any possible way by other events, for instance, any toss of a coin has exactly 50 percent probability of either being heads or tails. We can also speak of joint probability, that is, the probability of coming across more than one event, for example, what is the probability of the next three items retrieved from a set to be of particular values. We can calculate joint probabilities simply by multiplying the probabilities of each individual event together or, in mathematical notation, $P(A \text{ and } B) = P(A) \times P(B)$; here, $P(A)$ stands for the probability of the event A. Likewise, dependent events are events that depend on other events. For example, when we are iterating through a dataset rather than randomly asking numbers out of it, the probability of an item having a certain value does not depend solely on the number of its occurrences within this dataset, but also on how many times this value has been already retrieved and how many items are left in the dataset; in principle, we would have to recalculate its probability for the remaining dataset before we can calculate the actual probability. In the case of dependent events, we can speak of conditional probability, which stands for the probability of an event given some other condition. In mathematical terms, we can calculate the probability of A given B as $P(A \mid B) = P(A \text{ and } B) / P(A)$. By means of these simple rules, we can calculate the probability of complicated events and implement algorithms that target very specific cases. However, always bear in mind that probabilities are just indicators and at times can be erroneous—it could be that the next element in a dataset is one with a probability of only 0.1 percent.

Dealing with textual datasets

So far, we have only dealt with numerical datasets. It is, nonetheless, quite common to deal with a certain kind of non-numerical data, such as text-related data. Depending on the specifics of each application and what kind of information we are interested in extracting, dealing with textual datasets could be anything from extremely simple to overwhelmingly complicated. For instance, we can easily calculate how probable it is for a certain string to appear by means of counting their occurrences in a dataset, and then we can even calculate their probability distributions or map them to audio synthesis parameters. Yet, it would be extremely challenging, if not completely impossible with the current technology, to automatically synthesize the abstract of this chapter, provided the contents are available as a `String` object. Typically, performing sophisticated tasks with text involves stages, such as lexical analysis, syntactical analysis (or parsing), and semantical analysis, which are complicated enough to be the subject of dedicated books and hence, impossible to discuss in depth herein.

Let us consider a quite complicated, albeit very useful, **syntactical analysis problem**. Assuming that the whole text of this chapter is stored in some plain text file, how can we analyze it so that we can extract only those blocks of text that are valid SuperCollider code, and later, evaluate them at will? Given that SuperCollider is able to both parse and lexically analyze text formatted as valid SuperCollider code, all we need to do is analyze the text, identify such blocks, and encapsulate them as individual String objects; then, we can simply invoke their `interpret` instance method when we need to evaluate them. To actually implement such an algorithm, we need to describe it in a computer-understandable way that makes a code block different from irrelevant text. For our implementation herein, we will scan the text until we identify a parentheses followed by a blank character and a comment line delimiter (that is, a ' (//' character); then, all we need to do is find the match of this parenthesis, which signifies the end of the block. This is not necessarily a prerequisite for all of the valid code in SuperCollider; however, throughout this chapter, we have followed the convention that all standalone examples are formatted this way. We can implement a basic parentheses-matching algorithm if we simply increment a counter for every opening parentheses and decrement it for every closing one. When the counter equals zero, we know that we have found the ending of the code block in question. There is still a problem though since we have already used the ' (//' token in this chapter and outside the context of a code block (like in this very sentence), and since within the code examples, parentheses could be (are actually in this case) contained within instances of String, Symbol, Char or within comments that are neither necessarily matched nor signify the opening of a block of code.

For example in this chapter, we have intentionally enclosed those off-code-block appearances in quotes and made sure that the in-code ones are either matched or preceded by a quote or a $ symbol so that, with the addition of some simple rules, we can safely ignore them.

The code is as follows:

```
( // extract and evaluate code from text file
var file, path, text; // used to read the text from file
var cues; // of initial position of and '( //'
var chunks; // array with chunks of text containing potential code
var code;  // an array with the parsed code

path = PathName(thisProcess.nowExecutingPath).pathOnly ++
  "9677OS_08_chapterInPlainText.txt"; // the path to the file
file = File(path,"r"); // open for reading operations
text = file.readAllString; // read all text to a string
file.close; // close files
```

```
cues = text.findAll("( //");
 // find the positions of al occurences of '( //'
cues = cues.select{ arg index; (text[index - 1] != $') &&
  (text[index - 1] != $") };
 // remove all invalid parenthesis (ones preceded by ' or ")

(cues.size-1).do{ arg index;
  chunks = chunks.add(text[(cues[index] ..
  cues[index+1])].toString);
 // copy all text between subsequent cues and put it on chunks array
};
chunks = chunks.add(text[(cues.last .. text.size)].toString);
  // also add last chunk

chunks.do{ arg item, index; // for every chunk of text
  var counter = 0, position = 0, done = false;
  item.do{arg char,i; // for every character in chunk
  if (done.not) {
 // if not done, increment counter for every '('
  and decrement it for every ')'
  case
    {char == $( } { counter = counter + 1 }
    {char == $) } { counter = counter - 1 };
    if (counter == 0) {position = i; done = true;};
 // if counter equals 0, then the code ends at position i and the done
flag is set to true
  }
};
code = code.add(item[(0 .. position)].toString);
 // copy the parsed code to the code array
};

(code.size + " blocks of code have been successfully extracted from
text file").postln;
"Fourth code block will be now evaluated".postln;
code[5].interpret; // evaluate the sixth example
)
```

However simplistic this example is, having to correctly parse and evaluate the code sent to SuperCollider from some remote client is a real-life scenario, or at least something that I personally had to do many times in various projects. It does not necessarily make sense to do something like that, yet it is theoretically possible to even implement our own programming language within SuperCollider; this is so that the latter would correctly parse and translate it to its equivalent code that could later be evaluated by sclang.

Advanced mappings

In *Chapter 6, Data Acquisition and Mapping*, we demonstrated how we can essentially map any consecutive range to any other with respect to distribution curves. In this section, we will extend our arsenal of encoding techniques and introduce ourselves to how to implement complex and intelligent encodings.

Complex and intelligent encodings

There are situations wherein what we need is some kind of intelligence that will take the necessary decisions and select the appropriate process from a broader range of candidates in order to encode our data properly. To realize such mappings, we need some kind of mechanism that ensures the right decisions are taken and, of course, we need to define alternative behaviors. A simplistic way to implement decision-making algorithms would be by using test mechanisms and control flow structures, such as `if` or `case`. For the following simplistic example, assume that we want to sonify floating-point numerical values in the range of 0 to 1 so that they control oscillators that are either in a low (200 to 400) or in a high (2000 to 4000) frequency register. That is to say that our destination range is not continuous.

Consider this possible solution:

```
( // simple decision-making encoder
Server.default.waitForBoot({
  var data = Array.fill(100,{rrand(0,1.0)}); // our dataset
  var mappingFunc = { arg datum; // the mapping function
    if (datum<=0.5) { // if input is less than 0.5
      datum.linlin(0,0.5,200,400); // map linearly in the low register
    } {  // else map linearly to the high register
      datum.linlin(0.5,1.0,2000,4000);
    };
  };
  fork{loop{ // sonify dataset
    var freq;
    freq = mappingFunc.(data.choose);
    {SinOsc.ar(freq) * Line.ar(1,0,0.4,doneAction:2)}.play;
    0.5.wait;
  }};
})
)
```

This is a very simplistic case, of course, albeit it exemplifies how an algorithm can make decisions and is therefore a very primitive kind of artificial intelligence. In the next example, our algorithm is intelligent enough to dynamically make more sophisticated decisions and also with respect to analyzing the probability distribution of the remaining values in a dataset each time a value is used. The algorithm encodes data according to how probable it is to trigger certain frequencies in the output. Let us examine the various parts of the algorithm. The input data is just an integer's numerical values between 1 and 14 that we may use only once each. Then there are three possible ways to map the input data: frequencies that correspond to notes from the C major scale, with the most probable notes to be C, E, G, and B, frequencies that correspond to the Eb minor scale with the most prominent to be Eb, Gb, Bb, and Db, or just a random frequency. The seven most prominent values (the statistical head) will be mapped to the behavior *A*; then, if the probability of the next three consecutive values supposed to be within these seven values is greater than 60 percent, the rest of the values are all mapped to a random number, else they are mapped to the Eb minor group. To implement such an algorithm, and since the input range may vary, we need a function that will dynamically plug the input to the output range and perform the right encoding, as well as another function to calculate the probabilities and dynamically call the former with the right arguments.

In the core of our implementation, we have the following mapping function:

```
// mapping function
var mappingFunc = { arg data;
  var head, tail, prob, choice, freq, index;
  #head, tail = headTailFunc.(data);
 // calculate head and tails
  prob = probFunc.(data,head); // calculate the probality of the next
3 consecutive values to be in the head
  index = data.size.rand; // a random index in the dataset
  choice = data[index]; // pick a random value at index
  freq = if (head.includes(choice)) {
 // if chosen datum is in the head
    majorFunc.(head,choice); // call majorFunc
  } {
    if (prob > 0.29) {
 // else if the probability of the next 3 consecutive to be in the head
is more than 29%
      randFunc.(); // produce a random value
    } { // else
      minorFunc.(tail,choice); // call minorFunc
    }
  };
  data.removeAt(index); // remove datum from dataset
  freq; // return frequency
};
```

This mapping function relies on a series of auxiliary functions, such as headTailFunc (calculates the statistical head and tail), probFunc (calculates the probability of the next three consecutive values to be in the head), and a series of encoders, namely, majorFunc, randFunc, and minorFunc, which will return the actual frequency to play a sound. Since mappingFunc returns the frequency value, we can then simply play a sound like this:

```
// sound
fork{100.do{ var freq;
  freq = mappingFunc.(dataset); // encode data
  {SinOsc.ar(freq) * Line.ar(1,0,0.4,doneAction:2)}.play;
// play sound
  [0.5,0.25,1].wchoose([0.6,0.3,0.1]).wait; // wait
}};
```

As far as encoders are concerned, their implementation is rather trivial. The randFunc encoder simply returns a random frequency, while majorFunc and minorFunc first convert choice into a degree of the scale in question and then convert the latter into a value representing frequency.

The code for auxiliary functions is as follows:

```
// function calculate the head and Tail of the dataset
var headTailFunc = {
  arg data; // calculate head and tail of the dataset
  var head, tail, sorted;
  sorted = data.asBag.contents.asSortedArray.sort({arg a,b;
    b[1]<a[1]}).collect(_[0]);
// sort dataset so that the most probable values are first
  head = sorted.clipAt((0 .. 6));
// the 7 most probable values are the head
  tail = sorted.clipAt((7 .. 13)); // the rest are the tail
  [head,tail]; // return an array with the head and tail
};

  // function to calculate the probability of the next 3 consecutive
values to be in the head
var probFunc = { arg data, head;
  var prob;
  prob = head.sum(data.occurrencesOf(_)/data.size);
 // probability of next value to be in head
  prob.cubed;
 // return the probability of 3 consecutives values to be in the head
 };
```

The most complicated part is probably the highlighted line in the previous code, wherein we convert the dataset into `SortedArray`, containing all the different possible values the original dataset consisted of that are sorted by probability. The `asBag.contents` class will return an instance of `Dictionary`, wherein the possible entry in the original dataset points to its very number of occurrences. We then convert these keys/values pairs to duplets within `SortedArray`, where we apply our custom sorting algorithm so that the former is sorted with respect to how often an element occurs in the original dataset. The last part is to collect only these elements (and not their number of occurrences). The complete code for this example can be found online in the Packt code bundle for this book.

Neural networks

In computer science, **artificial neural networks (ANN)** are a fundamental machine-learning technique used whenever we want to achieve predictive modeling, adaptive control of some structure, and, in short, in all those cases when we want to grant our algorithm the ability to learn on its own according to data that is entered. Largely inspired by their biological equivalents, such networks operate via the flow of signals through individual neurons interconnected to greater structures rather than according to traditional computation paradigms. ANNs are extremely powerful and currently the only feasible way to solve certain kinds of problems. Typical examples are complicated pattern recognition or data classification problems. Consider, for example, a software application that identifies hand-written text and converts it into digital files. It is impossible to teach computers how to perform such a complex task, since we do not even properly understand how we do it ourselves. It is therefore impossible to describe an algorithm by traditional imperative or functional means. An ANN approach would be to provide the software with a large enough sample of successfully identified text and let it figure out by itself how to get there; or, in other words, let it learn.

There are several types of ANNs that may have either supervised, unsupervised, or reinforced learning abilities. We will limit our discussion here to arguably the simplest of all families of ANNs, namely, *feedforward neural networks*. Such a network typically consists of an *input layer*, an *output layer*, and an arbitrary number of layers in between that are broadly referred to as *hidden layers*. These layers consist of an arbitrary number of nodes, each of which is interconnected to the other according to the way each individual ANN is designed. Yet, in feedforward neural networks, as the name suggests and unlike biological neural networks, dataflow always occurs in one direction; there is no recursion. Such networks have the ability to learn; actually, we have to *train* them before we can use them. At any given time, the nodes in the hidden layers process the input by means of some *activation function* (there are several alternative ones) and with respect to a set of associated *weights* values. Initially, when the ANN is still young, these weights correspond to random values. During a single training cycle, also known as an *epoch*, we feed the network with input data, let them flow towards the output manipulated accordingly by the hidden layers, and then we compare the output with the desired one. The *error* is calculated and the information is back-propagated accordingly to update all the weights so that, when the input is fed back to the network, slightly better results can be achieved. Training a neural network typically involves several thousand epochs. Depending on the kind of problem, even millions or more of these epochs may be required, making the training a significantly time-consuming process for complex problems. Nevertheless, it does make sense to get into the trouble of training an ANN since, when done, we are left with a specialized brain capable of solving a very certain kind of problem, even if we cannot formalize a working algorithm ourselves.

Fortunately, a single-layered feedforward neural network is already being implemented for SuperCollider by *Nick Collins* and can be found in his SCMIR library that is available for download at `http://www.sussex.ac.uk/Users/nc81/code.html#SC`. Albeit rudimentary, NeuralNet is a fully functional ANN that we can use to add intelligence to our projects. The first thing to do is to let the class know the path of the `NeuralNet` unix executable file (bundled with the SCMIR library) like this:

NeuralNet.pathToNeuralNetBinary_("/Users/marinos/Library/Applicaton Support/SuperCollider/Extensions/SCMIRExtensions/scmirexec/NeuralNet") // set the path of the NeuralNet unix executable

This is not strictly necessary, but this way, we can use the `trainExt` method instead of the standard `train` method to train our network in significantly faster times. We only have to do this once, and the class will store information internally; even if we restart SuperCollider, `NeuralNet` will know where to find the appropriate executable. We can then create a new ANN simply proving the number of nodes for the input, hidden, and output layers, as well as the desired learning rate (typically in the range of 0.01 to 1.0) and a factor to initialize weights (they will be initialized to random values within a ± factor range).

To train the network, we need a sample, of course, which should be an instance of `Array`, containing instances of `Array` with the input and output values. Obviously, those arrays should contain as many elements as the corresponding number of nodes. We can then use `train` or `trainExt` to feed our data to our ANN, also providing a desired error and a maximum number of epochs. The network will keep iterating until the error in the calculations is less than the desired one or until the maximum number of epochs is achieved, posting its state at every stage so that we know what the final error is.

A simple example is as follows:

```
( // a simple Neural Network Example
var net, sample;
net = NeuralNet(2,20,1,0.01,1.0); // 2 ins, 1 out, 20hidden
sample = [ [[1,0],[1]], [[0.5,0.5],[0.5]], [[1,0.5],[0.5]],
  [[0,1],[0]] ]; // the sample
net.trainExt(sample,0.01,10000);
 // train over 10000 epochs or until the error is less that 0.01
// test
net.calculate([1,0]).postln;
net.calculate([0.5,0.5]).postln;
net.calculate([0,1]).postln;
net.calculate([0.75,0.25]).postln;
)
```

In my computer, the final iteration resulted in `Epoch: 19999, Error: 0.0221883`, so I know that this ANN is supposed to give acceptable results. And indeed, it maps, for instance `[ 1, 0 ]` to `0.92` and `[ 0.5, 0.5 ]` to `0.43`, which may not be the ideal `1` and `0.5` but are nevertheless very close and thus acceptable. At this stage, our ANN has already made extrapolations and identified some underlying pattern in our sample, and will map all the input values accordingly. We can see, for instance, that it mapped values `[0.5, 0.5]` to `0.18`, which does make sense since `[0.5, 0.5]` is supposed to result in `0.5` and `[0,1]` is supposed to result in `0`, and since `0.18` is indeed somewhere in between these values. This is the most intriguing aspect of ANNs; they tend to understand data in their own way without us having to explicitly explain (or even understand) the underlying patterns.

Arguably, for more complex problems, which could involve millions of epochs, we will most likely want to somehow save the neural network so we can use it again without having to train it from scratch. Luckily, `NeuralNet` provides us with invaluable methods to access the whole ANN's data specifications, including the weights, and to create new networks out of such specifications, namely, `getNN` and `newExisting` respectively. Also, note that `NeuralNet` will only operate with values in the zero to one range; therefore, we need to scale it accordingly in order to use it for other sorts of data.

Machine Learning is that branch of Artificial Intelligence that deals with the construction and study of systems that can learn from data.

A biological **neuron** (or neurone) is an electrically excitable cell that processes or transmits information in a human or in any other animal brain. In computer science, artificial neurons are mathematical functions conceived as the approximate models of biological neurons.

Automata

Automata is the plural of **automaton**, which in Greek stands for any kind of non-biological, self-operating being. When a program, or elements of it, operates on its own, either following finite behavior instructions by means of stochastic or probabilistic algorithms or by relying on some sort of artificial intelligence, we can speak of an automaton. Automata, in their various implementations, are fundamental parts of any **generative art** project, that is, art created partly or exclusively relying on some sort of autonomous, non-human controlled system. As far as mapping and visualization are concerned, whenever decisions and behaviors are performed intrinsically by our program, we can speak of a generative process that, by definition, involves some kind of automaton. Herein, we will pinpoint our discussion on the infamous cellular automata, while in the next chapter, we will discuss other kinds of automata as well.

Cellular automata

A **cellular automaton** comprises of an n-dimensional grid of *cells*, each of which has a certain *neighborhood* and may alternate between a finite number of *states* with respect to some set of *rules* usually considering the state of neighboring cells. On each generation, a cellular automaton will permute according to how each individual cell changes its state, thereby generating new patterns and structures dynamically. The initial pattern (which is also referred to as the *seed*) is of great importance and typically decisive of how the automaton will evolve over time. In the following example, we implement an elementary one-dimensional *Wolfram's* cellular automaton. Herein, our grid is merely a line of cells of 1-pixel width, each of which has a neighborhood of three pixels, the pixel itself, the pixel to its right, and the one to its left, and may alternate between two possible states represented by two possible colors. Each subsequent generation will be placed beneath the first one, which is placed on top, and will have its cells configured with respect to the previous one.

In detail, the state of each cell will be a function of the individual states of the cell that constituted the former's neighborhood in the previous generation. A rule in this context is a configuration of the possible outcomes of each possible combination. The possible states of a neighborhood of the three, wherein each cell alternates between two possible states, in binary notation would be: 000, 001, 010, 011, 100, 101, 111; here, 0 represents one of the two colors and 1 the other. We can then describe a rule as another binary number that holds the results for each of these configurations. For example, the rule 01011010 would mean that a cell having a neighborhood of 000 in the next generation will have a state of 0, a cell having a generation of 001 will have a state of 1, and so on. The following diagram describes the rule graphically (here black represents 0 and white 1):

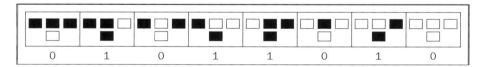

By the way, the number `01011010` corresponds to the decimal number `90` (which is arguably easier to remember). In SuperCollider, we can invoke `asBinaryDigits` on some decimal number to get an instance of `Array` containing the individual bits of its binary equivalent. Therefore, it does make sense to use decimals to describe rules. Configurations of eight bits may represent a maximum of 256 (including zero) different numbers. However, out of these possible rules, only a few will produce interesting results. Consider the following example wherein we use a 512-sized grid and we visualize/sonify the results of a cellular automaton. Sonification is done in the spectral domain using `pvcalc` to generate a spectrum with energy in those bins that correspond to a colored cell. Note that an instance of `Control` is used to allow instances of `Array` as arguments to our `Synth` class; the initial value of each parameter should be an instance of `Array` similar in size as that of the later passed as arguments; in our case, we will use instances of `Array` that comprise two 256-sized arrays, one for magnitudes and one for phases. Visualization is implemented using `Pen` to add one-pixel sized rectangles when a cell's value is one, else the background color is revealed.

The full code is as follows:

```
( // 1-dimension cellular automata
Server.default.waitForBoot({
  var synth; // a synth used later
  var ruleSet = [60,90,102,150].choose.asBinaryDigits;
 // randomly choose a rule and convert to an Array of binary digits
  var cells = Array.fill(512,{[0,1].choose([0.95,0.05])});
 // a random seed of mainly 0s and just a few 1s at random places
  var generateAccordingToRule = { arg a,b,c;
 // simply map each neighborhood state to each digit of our
rule, respectively
    case
    {(a == 0) && (b == 0) && (c == 0)} {ruleSet[0]}
    {(a == 0) && (b == 0) && (c == 1)} {ruleSet[1]}
    {(a == 0) && (b == 1) && (c == 0)} {ruleSet[2]}
    {(a == 0) && (b == 1) && (c == 1)} {ruleSet[3]}
    {(a == 1) && (b == 0) && (c == 0)} {ruleSet[4]}
    {(a == 1) && (b == 0) && (c == 1)} {ruleSet[5]}
    {(a == 1) && (b == 1) && (c == 0)} {ruleSet[6]}
    {(a == 1) && (b == 1) && (c == 1)} {ruleSet[7]};
  };
  var window = Window("1-dimension cellular automata",
    512@200).front.onClose_({synth.free;}); // our parent window
  var userView = UserView(window,
    512@200).background_(Color.magenta).animate_(true)
    .clearOnRefresh_(false).frameRate_(40).drawFunc_({
 // setup UserView and callback func
    var counter = userView.frame % 200;
```

```
    synth.set(\array, cells); // modulate synth
    512.do{ arg i;
      // first draw each cell
      if (cells[i].asBoolean) {
        Pen.fillColor_(Color.yellow);
        Pen.addRect(Rect(i,counter,1,1));
        Pen.fill;
      };
      // then calculate next generation
      cells[i] = generateAccordingToRule.value(cells.foldAt(i-
        1),cells[i],cells.foldAt(i+1));
    };
    // when we have reached the bottom start from scratch with a new
random rule and random seed
    if (counter == 0) {
      userView.clearDrawing; // clear previous contents
      ruleSet = [60,90,102,150].choose.asBinaryDigits;
 // randomly choose a rule and convert to an Array of binary digits

      cells = Array.fill(512,{0}); // an array of empty cells
      rrand(1,50).do{
 // add a random number of 1s at random places to achieve a random
seed
        cells[512.rand] = 1;
      };
    };
  });
  fork {  // sound
    SynthDef(\caSynth, { // synthDef
      var signal, array, magnitudes, phases;
      array =
        Control.names([\array]).kr(Array.fill(512,{0}))
        .clump(2).flop;
 // Control is used to allow an array to be passed as an argument
      magnitudes = array[0]; // read argument magnitudes
      phases = array[1]; // read argument phases
      signal = Silent.ar();
 // a silent signal since we will replace it
      signal = FFT(LocalBuf(512),signal); // FFT
      signal = signal.pvcalc(512,{
        [magnitudes,phases]; // manually set magnitudes and phases
      });
      signal = IFFT(signal); // inverse FFT
      Out.ar(0,signal!2);
    }).add; // add SynthDef
    Server.default.sync; // sync with Server
    synth = Synth(\caSynth); // start synth
  };
});
)
```

A still from this visualization is as shown in the following figure:

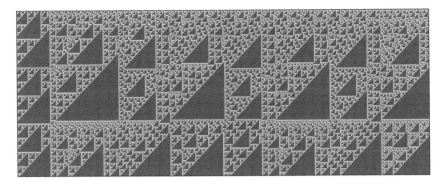

Cellular automata have been known since the 40s, primarily due to *Stanisław Ulam* and *John von Neumann* who first discovered and systematically studied them at the Los Alamos National Laboratory in New Mexico. It wasn't until the 70s, however, that cellular automata were popularized and exceeded narrow academic circles, primarily due to the infamous Conway's Game of Life, which we will soon discuss in more detail. A seminal work in the subject is *Stephen Wolfram's* 1,280-page book entitled *A New Kind of Science*. Wolfram argues that cellular automata are relevant to the study of biology, chemistry, physics, and several other branches of science. The entire book is freely available online at http://www.wolframscience.com/nksonline/toc.html

Game of Life

The infamous **Game of Life** is a two-dimensional cellular automaton originally devised by the British mathematician *John Horton Conway*. Here we have a two-dimensional grid, two-state cells (alive or dead in this context), and a 9-cell neighborhood (the cell in question and all its neighboring ones: up, down, left, right, and diagonal). There are four rules:

- **Loneliness**: Under this rule, any living cell with fewer than two living neighbors dies
- **Stasis**: Under this rule, any living cell with two or three living neighbors live on to the next generation
- **Over-population**: Under this rule, any living cell with more than three lives neighbors dies
- **Birth**: Under this rule, any dead cell with exactly three living neighbors becomes a living cell

What is particularly intriguing with the Game of Life is that there are certain patterns that will constantly oscillate between the same states, certain others will remain static, and certain others that appear as if they are moving. To implement a basic Game of Life, we will follow a similar approach as before; this time, however, we will use a two-dimensional array of cells:

```
cells=Array.fill(32,{Array.fill(16,{[1,0].wchoose([0.3,0.7])})});
```

It can also be implemented using the `updateCell` function instead of a ruleset as follows:

```
updateCell = {arg xIndex,yIndex;
 // function to count neighbours and update cells' state
  var neighbours = 0 ; // initial number of neighbours
  var state = cells[xIndex][yIndex]; // set current state
  var newState = state; // new state
  // first count neighbours
  [-1,0,1].do{arg i;
    [-1,0,1].do{arg j;
      neighbours = neighbours +
      cells.foldAt(xIndex+i).foldAt(yIndex+j);
    }
  };

  if (state.asBoolean) {neighbours = neighbours - 1};
 // if state is not 0, subtract cell's own state
  case  // calculate new state
  {state.asBoolean && (neighbours < 2)} {newState = 0}
 // it dies from loneliness.
  {state.asBoolean && (neighbours > 3)} {newState = 0}
 // it dies from overpopulation.
  {state.asBoolean.not && (neighbours == 3)} {newState = 1}; // birth
  // update
  cells[xIndex][yIndex] = newState;
};
```

And now using the same instance of `SynthDef` as before, we can proceed with th
`drawFunc` function like this:

```
.drawFunc_({ // setup UserView and callback func
var speed = userView.frame % 4;
synth.set(\array, cells.flatten); // sonify
cells.do{arg xItem, xIndex;  // for each cell
   xItem.do{arg yItem, yIndex;
      if (yItem!=0) { // draw current state
         Pen.fillColor_(Color.new255(214,176,49));
         Pen.addRect(Rect(xIndex*20,yIndex*20,20,20);
         Pen.fill;
      };
      if (speed==0) {updateCell.(xIndex,yIndex);};
// calculate and draw new state
   };
  };
});
```

The full code for this example can be found online at Packt's website in the book's
code bundle. A still from the visualization is as follows:

Summary

In this chapter, we dealt with more advanced topics, such as how to perform statistical analyses on datasets, how to parse textual information, how to perform intelligent encodings, and how to implement one-dimensional and two-dimensional cellular automata. The later are examples of generative systems that produce an audio and a video autonomously.

In the next chapter, we will implement a more sophisticated generative system as a case to demonstrate various design patterns and software architecture paradigms so that we are in position to properly design and implement code for more sophisticated systems.

9
Design Patterns and Methodologies

Being towards the end of this book and having discussed in depth how to address the various challenges of mapping and visualizing audio and data, as well as how to implement animation and audiovisual generative programs in SuperCollider, we will now dedicate this chapter to software architecture itself. We will discuss how to design, implement, and finalize a fairly involved example. With the introduction of miscellaneous common-design patterns, we will exemplify how certain problems can be cast as trivial, using the appropriate techniques. Of course, there is no single approach to software design and we may have to come up with our own particular designs for certain kinds of problems; nevertheless, the methodologies examined herein are very likely to occur in real-life projects since the kind of problems they solve are very common. It has to be said that this chapter does not pretend to be a treatise of design patterns, but rather it follows a pragmatic approach to demonstrate how we can solve real-life problems in efficient and elegant ways by means of using well-known computer science paradigms, even if in a broader or abusive fashion.

The topics that will be covered in this chapter are as follows:

- Understanding the Model-View-Controller paradigm
- Modeling objects with Environment
- Handling multiple files
- Designing patterns
- Understanding software agents
- Introducing actors

Blackboard

In this section we will examine the overall structure of our application and take decisions that impose a very particular kind of architecture on all the files and models we will be using. Prior to doing this, however, we need to discuss the details and the ramifications of our methodology.

Methodology

No programming language is an island, and SuperCollider is no exception. The chances are that, from a computer science perspective, the type of problems we are likely to encounter have already been encountered, studied, analyzed, and solved by others. More importantly, relevant algorithms, design patterns, and whole programming paradigms do exist and we can exploit them to accelerate our creativity. It must also be said that familiarizing oneself with such techniques has a significant psychological advantage too, as it fosters a more abstract way of thinking, wherein everything is solvable once we identify the kind of structural elements we will most likely use. Therefore, it is of fundamental importance, even for a casual programmer, to be aware of several recurring design patterns and strategies, so that they may efficiently and quickly conceptualize possible solutions to various problems they will encounter. Note that we have already encountered such patterns, for example, **Factories** or **Handlers**.

The most important stage in software design is to actually conceptualize and formally describe a possible solution. Sometimes, writing a code is the least significant task of a programmer these days and may only occupy a small fragment of his time. This may sound an exaggeration, yet, consider how trivial it is to write the necessary code for a series of short, well-documented, and scholastically-described algorithms and what it takes to arrive at this stage. As far as complex projects are concerned, once we have conceptualized and formally described a possible prototype, we are half way there. The first step to designing a project is to formalize and then study the requirements; these are descriptions of what our program should do (not *how*, but *what*) in the textual form. Without haste, we will proceed with a solid idea of a generative audiovisual application that combines several techniques we have encountered hitherto. Due to an obvious lack of inspiration, we will name our project as `Snakes`. The requirements for the project are as follows:

- Snakes must be a generative, audiovisual work featuring real-time, computer-generated audio and video.

- An initial number of intelligent kinematic snake-like creatures must wander freely in a two-dimensional space, also producing sound.

- Each creature must have a *body* (its visual representation), a *personality* (which could be either introvert or extrovert), a distinct *voice* (a unique sound-synthesis algorithm), and a very basic form of artificial intelligence (an ANN-driven *brain*).

- The snakes must largely be unaware of their spatial environment and should only be able to sense an evenly present datastream, which we will call `gestalt` (being largely influenced by *Greg Egan*'s novel *Diaspora*), which in essence is merely random data retrieved in real time from `www.random.org`.

- The snakes, being autonomous, intelligent creatures, should be able to interpret the data they sense, and decide how to move and vocalize at will.

Much like man, no snake is an island and whenever more than one society (may be, population is a better term when snakes are concerned) is formed, one creature affects the other. Therefore, every time a snake encounters another, there are three possible outcomes with respect to their personalities:

1. Whenever an introvert snake and an extrovert snake meet, the chances are that they fall in love and give *birth* to a new snake.

2. Whenever two introvert snakes meet, the chances are that they will simply ignore each other and hence *nothing* will happen; finally

3. Whenever two extrovert snakes meet, the chances are that they will fight each other, an action leading to mutual *death*.

However, life is strange and there is always a small possibility that things do not work out in this way, so our program should make sure that occasionally the results are different than those suggested.

The next step is to carefully consider what our program has to do, based on this description, and think of possible implementation designs. We should start with small steps and follow the **divide-and-conquer paradigm**, which dictates that we should break up complex problems to simpler, easier-to-solve ones. The idea is to have a rough plan, as soon as possible, which will lead to a working prototype. Always bare in mind that programming is an iterative process; in all probability, you will definitely revisit this design and revise it. The complexities of some problems cannot be fully appreciated, or even understood, until we actually start implementing them. Bear in mind that the code presented hereinafter was not written in this way. In fact, I typically had to revisit the original design and make minor modifications to compensate for various kinds of problems that emerged. Nevertheless, once there is an initial quasi-working design, it is easy to make it appropriate.

Model-View-Controller

If we reflect a bit on the previously mentioned requirements, we can identify certain objects that we will most likely need to design. In this world of object-oriented design, we should treat all key nouns and subjects, encountered in this text, as candidate objects to model, and all the key verbs as candidate methods. Even if it is highly unlikely that the final design will be a straightforward representation of these elements, it will be very close or will make significant use of them. For example, in our case here and even at such an early stage, studying these key elements (which are all highlighted in the preceding text will make it quite obvious that our solution will definitely feature a snake factory and that we will also need models for its various parts, such as the body or the brain).

It's also quite obvious that our project is quite involved and therefore, following the fundamental divide-and-conquer rule, we will have to break it into smaller parts, each of which will have a distinct role, and also implement some mechanism to permit interactions between them. Herein we will be using the infamous **Model-View-Controller** (**MVC**) architecture in a rather generalized and liberated fashion. The idea is to separate our program into three distinct parts: the **Model**, which will comprise all the models and factories for the various structures we will use in our program; the **View**, which will be the program's frontend, that is, that part of it responsible for delivering video and (in our case) audio; and the **Controller**, which will act as a mediator between the two when needed. That being so, the Controller is both—the Model's interface and its modulator. As we will see, the View and the Model should be distinct and isolated from each other, only providing public interfaces for the Controller to bridge them.

Typically, in an event-driven design, the Controller's role is twofold, to update the Model's behavior with respect to the View (with which the user interacts) and vice versa (since the changes in the Model should somehow reach the user). Our project is quite different, however, since we will not allow any user interaction (other than simply closing the animation window). Hence, in our case, the roles will be slightly different. The Controller's role would be only to update the Model's internal state (such as managing the population of snakes) and set up the View so that it visualizes this state. In any case, a question arises: who will take care of defining and initiating the Model, the View, and the Controller? This introduces us to another design pattern, that is, **Blackboard**, which will be our main, initial process that will take care of defining and launching the various parts of our program (Model, View, Controller) in the correct order.

The following figure exemplifies what we know until now about Snakes:

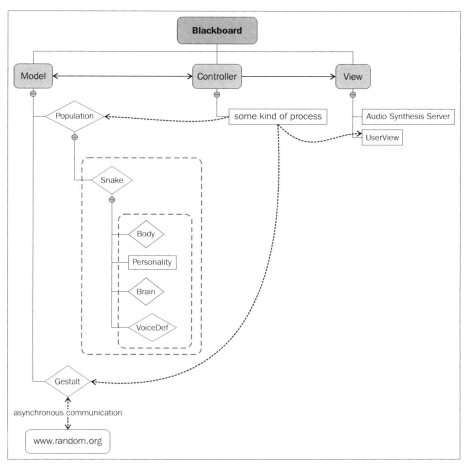

Notice that models are represented in diamonds in the preceding figure (contrasting simple variables, functions, and routines). In the figure, `VoiceDef` is used instead of `Voice`; this is because the unique synthesis algorithm in our requirement is apparently closer to a unique `SynthDef` object rather than a unique `Synth` object, as we will discuss later.

Handling multiple files and environments

Before discussing the specifics of the various parts, we need to start with Blackboard itself and consider the various kinds of actions it will have to perform. At this point, we can safely assume that our project will most likely be large enough to qualify to be split into multiple files. It does make sense, from a conceptual viewpoint, to keep at least the code for Blackboard, Model, View, and Controller in separate files. Note that all these parts are models themselves, yet we will need exactly one instance of every object in our project. Therefore, we only need to model them as singleton objects; no factory is needed; all we need to do is, evaluate the proper code once. By the way, since the whole idea of loading code from another file to the body of our program is similar (at least superficially) to the `#include` preprocessor directive in C/C++ languages, it does make sense (at least for me) to implement a similar class in SuperCollider, as shown in the following code:

```
Include { // class to evaluate code from other files.
  *absolute{ arg path;
    path.loadPaths; // evaluate code in file
  }

  *relative{ arg path;
    var pathToLoad = Document.current.dir +/+ path;
    pathToLoad.loadPaths; // evaluate code in file
  }
}
```

This `Class` does nothing more than invoking `loadPaths` on an absolute or relative path. However, in this chapter, we will prefer to include rather than load it since in our context it is conceptually more clear. Note that, as of writing, `Document.dir` was broken in the SCide and while it will probably be fixed in some future update, one may use `(PathName(thisProcess.nowExecutingPath).pathOnly` instead, as we did in the previous chapters. We can then include our various resources as shown in the following code snippet:

```
// include resources
Include.relative("Model.scd"); // evaluate code in Model.scd
Include.relative("View.scd");  // evaluate code in View.scd
Include.relative("Controller.scd"); // evaluate code in Controller.scd
```

In reality, we only plan to include the definitions for the various models and the helper functions that we will use in these files, yet it should be explicit that the `Include` class does not import definitions; rather, it evaluates the code in these files like a normal block of SuperCollider code. It is up to the designer (us) to reinforce any particular restrictions on what kind of code should be contained therein. It should also be highlighted that, from Blackboard's point of view, once a file is included, there should be a way to access the various definitions so that it is up to Blackboard to decide when and under what circumstances it will initiate and launch its elements. At least that is the architecture we are trying to reinforce herein.

Hitherto, we had used environment variables (the ones prefixed with ~) inside auxiliary files so that we can address these objects globally by means of their name. However, this is not the best approach, since the corresponding object would indeed be available globally to all the running programs, including the ones we try to isolate from each other (for instance, Model and View). Generally speaking, this is unacceptable, as it opens the door to all sorts of disasters (may be not the kind of disasters that actually kill people or ruin buildings, but nevertheless disasters that may cost hours of sitting miserably in front of the screen trying to locate some bug well hidden under several nested `Include`). Actually the problem is even more complicated than this; we need to ensure that only certain parts of our program are allowed to access certain others, and also need to ensure that we don't accidently use a name already reserved for something else, which may occur if we are including files that include other files. In other words, we need an additional safety net so that we can control who can access the code and under what circumstances.

Starting with the naming problem, wouldn't it be nice if we could still use simple names such as `draw`, `refresh`, `update`, and so on (instead of more explicit ones such as `someObjectDraw`), yet have them within a protected scope, that is, a **namespace**? Among other things, this would also guarantee that only those objects that have access to this scope may access these names. We can easily achieve these using `Environment`, as shown in the following code:

```
( // Blackboard.scd
var snakesProject = Environment.new;
snakesProject.use{
  // ------------------ LOAD RESOURCE ---------------------------
  Include.relative("Model.scd"); /* Model.scd is evaluated WITHIN this
(specific to this program) environment */
  ~model[\someElement].postln; // access elements within model
};
snakesProject[\model][\someElement].postln; /* the same but outside
the .use structure */
)
```

and also in the following code snippet:

```
// Model.scd
~model = Environment.new; /* define a new Environment WITHIN the
current environment */
~model.use{  // create elements WITHIN the model Environment
  ~someElement = "this is an element";
}
```

In SuperCollider, the ~ symbol is a shortcut for currentEnvironment.at, however, in our preceding example, the currentEnvironment object for all code within Model.scd is not the default one, but a new Environment object, accessible only to the code within the Blackboard.scd file (to be precise, only to that part of the code that is within parentheses). The preceding code demonstrates the syntax for accessing the internals of the model. Note that if need be, we can also have our code evaluated in some anonymous Environment object, using Environment. use directly. In this chapter we will elaborate on how we can create solid and safe object models using Environment, however, it should be noted that beyond all our precautions, SuperCollider will allow us to replace what key holds with something totally different, therefore, under any circumstances we should do so.

What we have achieved with this small trick may not be evident immediately, but if we consider it for a minute or two, we will soon realize that it is quite impressive. First of all, we now have a file-specific namespace nested within a program-specific namespace, and we can allow more nested layers if need be. In this way, within Model.scd, we can refer to our element simply as ~someElement, yet not err because Blackboard has to explicitly refer to it as ~model[\someElement]. So even if there was an element with the same name, for example, in View.scd (and if we follow the same architecture throughout of course) this would only be accessible with ~view[\ someElement]. More importantly, we have now achieved privacy for our Blackboard object. There is no way for anything other than Blackboard to access ~model[\ someElement], unless we explicitly include it there too. In this way, we know that nothing can mess up our program, unless we allow it to do so. There is also a third, equally if not more, important gain with this architecture that we will discuss later in this chapter.

 In object-oriented programming, the singleton pattern is a design pattern that restricts the instantiation of a class to solely one object.

Threads, semaphores, and guards

It does not take a lot for a project to involve tasks that depend upon other tasks or even situations of asynchronous communication wherein we should wait for something though we have no idea when it will end. Actually, in SuperCollider such cases are norms rather than exceptions. Considering that even if we were to finalize the simplest of all programs, namely the {SinOsc.ar}.play program, in SuperCollider, we would still have to ensure that it is evaluated once an instance of Server has been booted. Waiting until something is done before a block of code is always evaluated is necessary when sound is involved. Yet, even in cases wherein it is not strictly necessary, it is sometimes a nice idea. For example, in our Snakes project, it does make sense that first the View is initialized, then the Model, and then the Controller. It makes sense, because the Controller is a mediator to the Model and the View, therefore, they should already exist. Whether this is strictly necessary or not depends upon the specifics of our code; it would be a nice idea nevertheless, to always ensure the parts of our program are initiated in this order. The same applies for the various internal elements of these structures; certain elements are likely to depend on the creation of others. In other words, we need a solid synchronization mechanism.

We have already demonstrated how we can synchronize with asynchronous events while: adding SynthDefs to Server, waiting for it to boot, reading files, invoking Unix commands, or even waiting for triggers or messages via OSC or MIDI. Now we need to discuss ways in which we can synchronize custom blocks of code with each other. We can easily do it since SuperCollider is a multithreading environment that allows us to divide the flow of our programs into different threads of execution. Note that by multithreading, herein, we are not referring to our computer processor's multithreading capabilities (even if SuperCollider tries to take advantage of them implicitly); we are simply referring to how we can implement parallelism in our programs by means of several pseudo-simultaneous threads (we do not need to be concerned with what this may mean). Actually this is very typical, we do it all the time in SuperCollider and we even do more complicated stuff, such as sharing data between different instances of Thread. Consider that in essence, every instance of Task or Routine is a different thread (by the way, they are both instances of Thread, which is an **abstract class**).

Many of those who are new to SuperCollider will typically have their threads wait for an arbitrary amount of time whenever they want them to sync with something, so that they allow it to realize its job. Apart from not being elegant at all, there are obvious drawbacks in this approach since in all cases we will either wait more or less than the actual need. Luckily there are other elegant ways around synchronization problems. Computer science formalizes two possible solutions with the **Semaphore** and the **Condition** design patterns. Luckily, both are already implemented in SuperCollider, so we can use them directly. If we want to allow only a specific number of concurrent instances of Routine, we can use instances of the Semaphore class to control them. More typically, however, we will want to wait for something before we proceed. We can achieve this using the Condition class.

Consider the following example:

```
( // Sync with Condition
var condition = Condition(false);
fork{
  condition.wait;
  // wait for the other thread to finish before you start
  "Thread A: I'm running now, yeah!".postln;
};
fork{
  "ThreadB: Let's imagine that I have to do sth asynchronously
  that will last for 10 seconds".postln;
  10.wait;
  condition.test_(true); // set to true
  condition.signal; // notify anyone interested
}
)
```

Therefore our Blackboard can be implemented as follows:

```
( // Blackboard.scd
var snakesProject = Environment.new;
snakesProject.use{
  // ------------------ LOAD RESOURCES ---------------------------
  Include.relative("Model.scd");
  Include.relative("View.scd");
  Include.relative("Controller.scd");
  // -------------------- Conditions ---------------------------
  // flags to control the flow of execution
  ~viewReady = Condition(false);
  // etc ...
  // ------------------ INIT FUNCTIONS ---------------------------
```

```
  // initiate View
  ~initView = {
    "Attempting to initate View".postln; // notify system
    ~view[\init].value; // initiate View
    ~view[\initiated].value.wait; // wait for it to be initialized
    "Done initiating View".postln; // notify system
    ~viewReady.test_(true);  // change condition when done initiating
    ~viewReady.signal; // propagate change
  };


  // also initiate the Model and Controller here ...

  // ------------------ LAUNCH PROGRAM  -------------------------
  fork {  // initiate the various parts of the program
    ~initView.value;   // initiate View
    ~viewReady.wait;   // proceed only when done !
    // etc ...
    "All parts of the program have been initiated succesfully!".
postln;
    "Now the program will start !!".postln;
  };
};
)
```

The complete code can be found online in this book's code bundle. All are pretty straightforward. However, there are a couple of things that need to be clarified. First, notice how Blackboard imposes a particular design on the levels below it. Model, View, and Controller should all implement an init method, which should return an instance of Condition to indicate that they are successfully initiated. It's up to Blackboard whether it should exploit this feature or not, but generally speaking it should. Blackboard's role is simply to redirect the initiation to each corresponding object and then it's this particular object's responsibility to initiate itself properly and notify Blackboard when done. Typically we will apply the same methodology when needed to ensure that the various parts of Model, View, and Controller objects are initiated in the right order. Also note that we have added notification messages everywhere so that in the case of errors (which, as we already know, happen more than often while developing code) we know exactly in what part of our program it occurred and therefore, we can easily identify, isolate, and fix it. Again we should follow the same style throughout all our objects to facilitate debugging.

 An abstract class is a class that is not supposed to be instantiated, but is rather designed to be specifically used as a base class for other subclasses to inherit from it.

The View

We are now ready to proceed with our View. In our case, the View is not only responsible for what we see, but also for all those parts of our program that constitute its output. Since `Snakes` is an audiovisual work, the View should be responsible for constructing and holding an instance of `Window` with a properly configured instance of `UserView`, as well as for initiating the sound synthesis engine, that is an instance of `Server`. Note that the View is not just a file packed with code for decompressing Blackboard. It is an object of its own sake and has certain tasks and responsibilities to carry out, also reinforced by Blackboard's requirement that it should implement an `init` method and an `initiated` member.

Clients and interfaces

A properly designed object should only expose the parts of itself that the other parts of the program need to access, and nothing more. Moreover, it should only expose these parts in a safe way, that is, in a way that does not allow third parties to alter their internal structure, thus fostering **encapsulation**. Every decent, well-designed object should communicate with the world exclusively through a specialized interface. We have already discussed interfaces in *Chapter 4, Vector Graphics*, wherein we highlighted the importance of keeping certain things private. This is a fundamental principle that we should always attempt to maintain at all costs. Nothing should be exposed unless completely necessary, and what is exposed should only be exposed through some specialized interface.

The interface's task is twofold. On the one hand it isolates the internals of an object so that they cannot be accidentally or erroneously modified in unwanted ways. For example, our Controller will have to control the way certain elements of View behave, but not these very elements per se. If the View did expose the underlying `UserView` or `Window`, it would introduce a vulnerability to the stability of our program, since it would make it possible to break View's implementation from within the Controller. This is the way to disaster as it could cause the whole program to crash, simply because of a typo. We will see later how to solve this particular problem efficiently and safely. Now we need to consider the second fundamental task of an interface: to isolate the internals of an object in order to hide their complexities. This is also an encapsulation, but of a different and more subtle form. Consider our View object; all we want it to do is just initiate itself, provide an instance of `Condition` so that its clients know, and a couple of methods to change its behavior. This means, all the underlying tasks of constructing and setting up the various GUI elements need not be exposed as objects or as information. In other words, the interface should be simple and easy to use from its client's perspective.

So who is this client? In our case we have two clients, Blackboard and the Controller, as no one and nothing else is supposed to ever use the View. But generally speaking, the client of an object is anything or anyone who might use it. This includes actual human beings as well as pieces of software and even hardware. Note also that the whole idea of creating abstract models is to also foster code reusability; subsequently an object's client may end up being something/someone completely different than what/who we had in mind while designing the interface. It is also important to realize that, from the client's perspective, an object's interface should be as simple and as conceptually straightforward as possible and thus it should completely hide all the intrinsic mechanics of the object and the complexities of its implementation. The interface should reflect the client's desires and not the logic of its implementation. On account of that, some simple rules follow. Nothing should mess up with the internal state of an object. Do not return objects directly, rather provide an **accessor** (sometimes also referred to as **getter**) method that returns these objects or their value. The actual objects should remain encapsulated within the original object, therefore ensuring it is protected. Notice that this is why in the preceding Blackboard's code we call `.value.wait` on `~view[\iniated]` and not simply `.wait`, because `~initiated` is an instance of `Function` returning a `Condition`. This is safer than returning the instance of `Condition` itself. Likewise, if we want to allow the modification of some object, we should do this again with specialized methods (referred to as **modifiers** or **setters**) that should ideally also ensure that their argument satisfies a certain criterion (such as being of the right type or in the right range of values) before actually modifying something. Other than this, we should simply make sure that our interfaces are easy to use and easy to understand.

Coming back to our View object, its public interface should feature, apart from the standard in our design `init` and `initiated` methods, just a `setDrawFunc` method and a `setOnCloseFunc` method to set up our `UserView` object's `drawFunc` function and the `onClose` handler of our parent `Window` object respectively.

> In object-oriented programming, encapsulation is an attribute of object design wherein a class' data members remain intrinsic and hidden within the object itself and are generally accessible only to other members of the same class and their respective subclasses.

Implementation

Languages such as C++, Java, or Objective-C, for example, are fundamentally structured around the schism between an interface and its implementation and hence provide special keywords to define whether some element is publicly accessible or is to be kept private. In SuperCollider, private membership is not explicitly supported in any object, yet it can be easily implemented, as we demonstrated in *Chapter 4, Vector Graphics*, wherein we designed our first Factory. The idea is simple; we can use variables with a limited scope, therefore, inaccessible to anything outside this scope, and have our public methods act as a bridge towards them. SuperCollider will automatically destroy variables and their contents once they are out of scope and once there is nothing pointing (or referring, if you prefer) at them. Consider the following code snippet:

```
// some object in a separate scd file
var someVariable = 30;
var someFunction = {someVariable = 50;};

~someObject = Environment.new;
~someObject.use{ // public interface
  ~accessor = {
    someVariable.postln;
    someFunction.value;
    someVariable.postln;
  }
}
```

When we use `Include` to evaluate this file from another file we can only access its interface that is, `~someObject [\accessor]`, through which we can access (but not set) `someVariable` and `someFunction`, which can be understood as existent private member variables of `someObject`. These are still referred to in our program even if they are technically just remnants of ordinary variables that have gone out of scope.

Note that the implementation of an object is fundamentally different in scope than its interface and therefore, not the same guidelines apply; quite the contrary actually. Herein our target group is programmers (which could be just us really, albeit this is not a less serious situation). Bare in mind that we can never tell the scope of our code and that, even if our objects are project specific, we may quite often return to them to make them appropriate for some other project. Let's take the View as an example; the way we will implement it here is of potential use to any kind of audiovisual project, therefore, we should try our best to keep it easily configurable. Subsequently, it is always a good thing to be scholastic in writing both meaningful and useful comments and, if necessary, more sophisticated textual descriptions of our code.

A possible implementation of View along with its public interface is shown in the following code:

```
// View.scd
// ----------------- IMPLEMENTATION ---------------------------
var parentWindow, userView; // graphics elements
var serverReady = Condition(false); // a condition
var guiReady = Condition(false); // a condition
var drawFunc = {}; // default drawing function
var initiated = Condition(false); // condition to notify clients


// --- private helper functions -----

var bootServer = { // function to boot the server
  "Attempting to initiate the sound synthesis engine".postln;
  Server.default.waitForBoot({
    "Sound synthesis engine is running !".postln;
    serverReady.test_(true);  // change condition to proceed
    serverReady.signal; // propagate change
  });
};

var makeGui = {  // create GUI elements
  { // defer
    "Attempting to create the animation window..".postln;
    parentWindow = Window.new("Snakes Project",
    640@640,false).front;
    userView = UserView.new(parentWindow,parentWindow.bounds);
    userView.background_(Color.black).animate_(true).frameRate_
    (30).clearOnRefresh_(false).drawFunc_({
      // add trailing effect
      Pen.fillColor_(Color(0,0,0,0.5)); // a transparent black
      Pen.addRect(Rect(0,0,640,640));   /* create a semi-transparent
rectangle to cover previous contents (for trailing effects) */
      Pen.fill; // draw rectangle
      /* call custom drawingFunc with userView.frame passed as
argument */
      drawFunc.value(userView.frame);
    });
    guiReady.test_(true); // set initiate flag to true
    guiReady.signal; // notify anybody interested
    "The animation window has been created!".postln;
  }.defer;
};
```

```
var initFunc = { fork { // initate View
  bootServer.value; // boot server
  serverReady.wait; // wait for Server to boot
  makeGui.value; // createGUI elements
  guiReady.wait; // wait for Window to be made
  initiated.test_(true); // set initiate flag to true
  initiated.signal; // notify anybody interested
}};

var setDrawFunc = { arg f; /* set a custom Function as the drawing
Function */
  drawFunc = f;
};

var setOnCloseFunc = { arg f; /* set a custom Function as the drawing
Function */
  parentWindow.onClose_(f);
};

// ------------------ PUBLIC INTERFACE ----------------------------
~view = Environment.new;
~view.use{ // public interface of View
  ~init = initFunc;
  ~initiated = {initiated};
  ~setDrawFunc = setDrawFunc;
  ~setOnCloseFunc = setOnCloseFunc;
};
```

Strategies and policies

View's implementation hereinbefore is very straightforward. Let us focus on the following parts of the code:

```
.drawFunc_({
  //.. trailing effects implementation
  drawFunc.value(userView.frame);
});
```

and

```
setDrawFunc = { arg f; // set a custom Function as the drawing
Function
  drawFunc = f;
};
```

This may seem quite uncanny to some, but it perfectly exemplifies the spirit of this whole chapter. It is straightforward for the client, elegant for the programmer, and more importantly, as safe as it gets. To appreciate why, consider an alternative as shown in the following code snippet:

```
setDrawFunc = { arg f; // set a custom Function as the drawing
Function
  userView.drawFunc_({f});
};
```

This may seem fine, but let us have a second look. There are at least three problems with this code. First, it would be up to the Controller to implement the trailing effects, yet it is not really its role to control such a kind of decorative effect, it's the View's. Doing so would be conceptually wrong and would mess up with the architecture of our program. Second, in this way we cannot access `userView.frame` from within our function, therefore, we would have to define some sort of a custom `getFrameCount` accessor, which may indeed be something trivial, and yet, since the place where we would use the counter is inside our function, we may complicate the kind of code our client should write. This is not an elegant approach. By the way, now that we are in the last chapter, you will probably agree with me that elegance, as far as programming is concerned, is the door to both aesthetic and pragmatic rewards. The most important argument against such a design, however, is that the `setDrawFunc` setter in the preceding code still returns `userView` implicitly, which is a dangerous practice. For instance:

```
~view[\setDrawFunc].value({/* some drawing function here */}).postln;
```

We could of course have our function return something different, but what and why? Now consider our solution again. Here, `setDrawFunc` returns just a function, which happens to be exactly the function we want to use, so there is absolutely no way we can use it do something different; `userView` is inaccessible. Since `userView` calls our custom `f` within its `drawFunc` function, we can still have it run the View-specific code before, or even after, the `Function` object is evaluated. The roles of the various objects are not violated this way and View's clients can be limited only to what is conceptually meaningful. And finally, we can now access the invaluable `userView.frame` counter from within `drawFunc` in a very elegant way (which also happens to be quite idiomatic in SuperCollider and therefore, is preferred). Now we can do things as follows:

```
~view[\setDrawFunc].value({arg counter; /* use counter here */ });
```

This can be done easily without violating View's privacy, as there's still no way to access userView externally. Even if the function we provide to setDrawFunc is erroneous and causes an error, it will keep on evaluating without affecting the View (unless the error is so severe that the whole interpreter crashes), therefore, we will even have a chance to fix things, at least in theory. By the way, we will not use this counter in our Snakes project, but it's a feature worth having, and also makes the View a nice candidate to be considered in the context of other projects.

The Model

The Model is probably the most complicated object in our project, since it holds all the custom models we will use in Snakes. We need to design two singleton objects, namely population and gestalt. Both are singleton because in Snakes we need exactly one instance of both. We also need snakeFactory to construct snake objects. However, as we have already discussed, the latter consists of several parts, therefore, we need to model each of them as well and implement all the necessary factories, since we will need more than one. Because of its complexity, we will only give excerpts of the code here; the complete Model.scd file can be found online in this book's code bundle.

Aggregates and wrappers

A snake entity is complex, or what we call in computer science, an **aggregate** (or a composition), since they consist of various dissimilar parts. For instance, they have body, personality, brain, and voiceDef associated with them. voiceDef stands for a unique sound synthesis algorithm for each snake, which is the basis of its voice. In essence, voiceDef is an instance of SynthDef, therefore, the task of voiceDefFactory is to algorithmically create a new and a unique SynthDef object. For example:

```
// -- voiceDefFactory --
var voiceDefFactory = { // voiceDef should be a unique SynthDef
  var uniqueName = Main.elapsedTime.asSymbol;
  // use elapsedTime as a uniqueName identifier
  /* create a unique SynthDef by means of choosing through possible
UGens */
  var voiceDef = SynthDef(uniqueName,{ arg freq = 200;
    var sound = [SinOsc,LFSaw,LFTri,LFPulse].choose.ar(freq);
    sound = [SinOsc,Saw,Pulse].choose.ar(sound.range(freq*0.5,freq));
    sound = sound *
    [
    [SinOsc,Saw,Pulse].choose.ar(rrand(freq/2,freq*2)),
      [WhiteNoise,BrownNoise].choose.ar(rrand(0.2,0.8))
    ].choose;
```

```
    sound = sound * EnvGen.kr(Env([0,1,0],[1,1])
    .circle,timeScale:rrand(0.1,3));
    Out.ar(0,Pan2.ar(sound,1.0.rand2)*0.4);
  });
  voiceDef; // return synthDef
};
```

The code is quite straightforward; each time the factory is called, it will create an instance of `SynthDef` by means of choosing random candidate UGens from its list, and combining them. We already have `body`; remember that we implemented a similar factory in *Chapter 5, Animation*. Yet, from this chapter's perspective there are certain problems with this model. In particular, its interface is not in accordance to the guidelines we have set hereinbefore in several respects; the most important being that it violates privacy. In such cases, and to avoid rewriting the whole factory, we can simply wrap our body with a new object that will guarantee a new, and better in some respects, interface to our old object. Such objects are called **wrappers**. For example:

```
// -- bodyFactory -
var include = Include.relative("9677OS_kinematicSnakeFactory.scd");
// include the kinematic snake factory
var bodyFactory = { arg position = Point(100,100),
  numberOfSegments = 20, length = 10, width = 30;
  var bodyWrapper; /* a wrapper around the body to implement a new
interface */
  var colorFunc = { // a function returning a function to use as color
    var a = rrand(0.4,1); // a random coefficient
    var b = rrand(0,1); // another random coefficient
    [ {arg i; Color.new(a,b,i)}, {arg i; Color.new(i,a,b)},
      {arg i; Color.new(a,i,b)}, {arg i; Color.new(b,a,i)},
      {arg i; Color.new(b,i,a)}
    ].choose; // choose a random colorFunc
  var body = ~snakeFactory.value(numberOfSegments, length, width,
colorFunc.value);
  body.refresh(position); /* set position (the old interface wouldn't
do that directly) */

  // our new public Interface
  bodyWrapper = ( // snake body's  public interface
    getPosition: {body.position},
    refresh: { arg self, position;
      body.refresh(position);
    },
    draw: { body.draw}
  );
  bodyWrapper; // return the body object
};
```

Notice that we use the `kinematicSnakeFactory.scd` file (which we introduced in *Chapter 5, Animation*) that contains the definition of the original `~snakeFactory` directory. Generally speaking, it is better to include such dependencies in the beginning of our files (as we do in the proper `Model.scd` file found online) so that we can tell immediately if a file depends on others. The reason we assign the result of `Include` in a variable is not because we plan to use it, but simply to avoid breaking our particular style here, wherein we introduce variables with their definition rather than having them all grouped in the beginning (which I personally find counterintuitive).

As far as `personality` is concerned, we do not need to make a new object; we can simply use an instance of `Symbol` to declare whether the snake is `introvert` or `extrovert`. The `brain` could be ANN trained, using a random input and a provided numerical rule (which we will call `brainSeed`) as the desired output. A possible design is shown in the following code snippet:

```
// -- brainFactory --
var brainFactory = { arg brainSeed = [ [1,1],[0,0] ];
// create a brain !
  var ann =  NeuralNet(4,20,2,0.01,1.0); // a primitive brain
  var sample = brainSeed.collect{arg i;
  [ Array.fill(4,{rrand(0.0,1.0)}), i  ]
    }; /* pairs of random values are mapped to each of the brainSeed
    elements */
  "Now creating a new artificial brain for the snake!".postln;
  ann.trainExt(sample,0.1,1000); // train network
  ann; // explicitly return ann
};
```

Software agents

And now that we have all its parts ready, we can finally code `snakeFactory` in the following manner:

```
// -- snakeFactory --
var snakeFactory = { arg position, numberOfSegments, length, width,
  brainSeed, gestalt;
  // create the various parts out their factories here
  // ...
  var initRoutine = fork { // setUp snake !
    /* use a routine and a condition to check if the brain has been
trained here */
    // ...
    // add voiceDef, sync to the Server and start a voice here ...
    // now our little snake is ready to start a life on its own !!
```

```
life = fork { loop{
  var value, newPosition, newFrequency;
  value = brain.calculate(gestalt.value);
  // first interpret gestalt
  // decide towards where to move and do it !
  newPosition = body.getPosition.translate(value.linlin(0,1,-
  10,10).asPoint); // newPosition is relative to old position
  newPosition = newPosition.wrap(0,640);
  body.refresh(newPosition); // set new position
  // decide what to say and speak!
  newFrequency = value.sum.linlin(0,2,100,3000);
  voice.set(\freq, newFrequency);
  1.0.rand.wait; // move every random amount of seconds
  }};
  snakeReady.test_(true); // change flag now that snake is ready
  snakeReady.signal; // propagate change to anyone interested
};
var killFunc = {
// kill snake: free voice Synth and stop life Routine here
};
var snake = ( // snake's  public interface
  getPersonality: { personality }, // return personality (a
Function)
  getPosition: { body.getPosition },
  // return position (a Function)
  kill: killFunc,
  draw: {body.draw},
  isReady: {snakeReady}
);
snake; // return snake
};
```

Again, only the most important parts are shown here; the complete code can be found online in this book's code bundle. During this stage of object modeling, it is essential to write testing code for all of our objects so that we know whether they behave the way they should, before we proceed. In this way we will save debugging time in the long run.

The `snake` objects generated by our factory are quite particular; more than being simply complex aggregates made from various other parts, they are also alive! They are living entities that move and produce sounds on their own, being driven by some internal motor (their brain). The latter may be primitive, but it is nevertheless some form of intelligence that casts our snakes as autonomous. During their lifetime, our snakes will regularly call `value` on `gestalt`. This is its only means to probe and interpret its surroundings and behave according to what it perceives. Subsequently, a `snake` object once created, acts on its own, without the intervention of any client being necessary. Such elements that are independent, autonomous, and act on their own are called **software agents**. (By the way, nowadays software agents are to be found everywhere in computing, especially on the World Wide Web where they probe for information of all sorts, for example, while indexing websites on behalf of search engines and similar applications). So, since our snakes are autonomous and since clients should not directly interact with them, how do we control them? Well, we do not need to control them, at least that was the idea in the first place; remember our original requirements? The only thing we need to do is make sure we can kill existent snakes or spawn new ones when needed; this is the only rule of the game. Note that a snake's public interface provides accessors for `position` and `personality` so that we can later use them to perform all the necessary tests and decide under which particular circumstances should a particular snake be killed or kept alive.

Introducing software actors and finalizing the model

It will be the task of `population` to kill or spawn snakes when needed. A `population` is really nothing more than a frontend to an instance of an `Array` containing `snakes` but with a proper public interface so that nobody can access the `snake` object themselves. The code is trivial so it will not be discussed here. An instance of `population` is a special kind of object too. It is responsible for managing the life and death of other objects, therefore, it is a kind of **Collection** (which is a well-known design pattern in SuperCollider), yet, unlike most collections we normally use, it also has complex responsibilities and is capable of communicating with its elements through their public interface. Instances of `population` will be present constantly from the beginning until the end of our program, and will wait for their client (it will be the Controller really) to tell it what to do. Then and only then, will it perform some action. Such kinds of objects are sometimes referred to as **software actors**, and are different from agents as actors must be explicitly asked to do something before they do it. In other words, an actor will not perform an action autonomously. (I'm really not sure if this is the case with human actors, by the way.)

The last element of our Model is the `gestalt` object, which is a singleton object responsible for retrieving data from `www.random.org` and distributing them at will. We will access the data using the asynchronous `unixCmd` and a temporary file, as we did in the example in *Chapter 7, Advanced Visualizers*. The code for `gestalt` is also trivial and will not be discussed here. To finish our Model, all we need is its `initFunc`, which will initialize the Model and its public interface. Initialization simply retrieves the first chunk of data from `www.random.org` and creates an initial population of 10 snakes. The latter is pretty straightforward and allows its clients to only access `initFunc`, `initiated` `Condition`, and the public interfaces of `population` and `gestalt`. For example:

```
// ------------------ PUBLIC INTERFACE --------------------------
~model = Environment.new; // define a new environment
~model.use{ /* notice that there is no way to directly access
snakeFactory */
  // snake objects can be accessed indirectly only
  ~init = initFunc;
  ~initiated = {initiated};
  ~population = population;
  ~gestalt = gestalt;
};
```

The complete `Model.scd` file can be found online in the code bundle of this book.

The Controller

Having implemented the View and the Model, we now need to ensure that they communicate with each other and that their elements are properly updated. The Controller is a simple object, at least when compared to the Model. It only has two basic responsibilities: to be the mediator between the Model and the View, and to update the state of the Model itself according to the rules that govern our system. The Controller will consist of the standard `init` and `initiated` (in our design) members as well as the necessary `gestaltUpdate` and `populationUpdate` agents. Note that the Controller needs access to both the Model and the View, therefore, when we initialize it, we should make sure we assign the latter to variables accessible to all elements of the Controller.

Game of Life

In essence, Snakes is a kind of Game of Life. The population changes according to a very specific set of rules that determine what will happen when two snakes meet. Keeping in my mind the result of what will happen when two particular snakes meet and our requirements, it is easy to implement the following code:

```
// ------- Rules -------
var resultOfEncounterFunc = { arg personalityA = \introvert,
personalityB = \introvert;
  var result, scenarios;
  scenarios = [\love, \nothing, \death]; // the posible results
  case
  {personalityA != personalityB} {
// if an introvert and extrovert meet
    scenarios.wchoose([0.8,0.1,0.1])
// they will most likely love each other
  }
  { (personalityA == personalityB) && (personalityA == \introvert) } {
    // if they are both introvert
    scenarios.wchoose([0.1,0.8,0.1])
// the chances are that they will ignore each other
  }
  { (personalityA == personalityB) && (personalityA == \extrovert) } {
    // if they are both extrovert
    scenarios.wchoose([0.1,0.1,0.8])
// the chances are that they will kill each other
  };
};
```

Of course we will need an ever-present background agent to observe and regulate population according to these rules:

```
// ------- gameOfLife -------
var gameOfLifeFunc = {
  populationUpdate = fork{loop{ // population updating agent
    var killIndices = Set.new; /* if we remove some item while in the
loop the next iterations while be affected so we will indices here
and kill snakes afterwards (we use a set so that we don't attempt to
delete the same element twice) */
    var spawnNewPositions = Set.new;
    // nested do loops to test each element with each every other one
    model[\population].getNumberOfSnakes.value.do{ arg indexA;
      model[\population].getNumberOfSnakes.value.do{ arg indexB;
        if (indexB > indexA) { /* to avoid testing an item with
itself, as well as with items it has already being tested */
          var dist = model[\population].getPosition(indexA).
dist(model[\population].getPosition(indexB)); // calculate distance
          if (dist < 10) { // if distance is less than 25 pixels
            var action = resultOfEncounterFunc.
(model[\population].getPersonality(indexA),
model[\population].getPersonality(indexB));
            // dist.postln;
            ("Two snakes have encountered.. the result is: " +
            action).postln;  // notify of the result of encounter
            case
            {action == \love} {
// spawn a new snake 30 pixels away from the first one
              spawnNewPositions =
              model[\population].getPosition(indexA) + 30;
            }
```

```
              {action == \nothing} { /* do nothing */ }
              {action == \death} { // keep indices to kill later
                killIndices = killIndices.add(indexA);
                killIndices = killIndices.add(indexB);
              };
          }
        }
      }
    };
    // kill snakes
    killIndices.do{ arg item;
      model[\population].kill(item);
    };
    // spawn new
    spawnNewPositions.do{arg position;
      model[\population].spawnNew(position,
        25,rrand(5,15),rrand(5,30), Array.fill(rrand(1,4), {
          Array.fill(2,{rrand(0,1.0)})}),
        {model[\gestalt]. returnDatum}).wait;  // remember it returns
a condition !
    };

    0.1.wait; // wait 2 seconds (so that actions do not occur
immediately)
  }};
};
```

Do not worry about the fact that `model` stands for nothing here; we will make sure it points to the actual Model when we initialize the Controller, which, if we follow our design throughout, is guaranteed to happen before we actually call `gameOfLifeFunc`. Other than this, there are some complexities in this code, the major one being how to test the positioning of one snake against all others. These sort of problems are fundamental in programming, generally speaking. One thing is sure: in a process looping every 0.1 seconds we do not want to perform more tests than absolutely required. The implementation above is not optimal, yet it does the job in an easy-to-understand way. In principle we nest a full iteration over all the `snake` objects into another, so we can test the positioning of each `snake` with every other, but we only perform tests when the index of the latter is greater than that of the first. In this way we ensure that we do not test the position of a `snake` with itself and also guarantee that we don't perform the same test twice. By the way, we could have implemented the same code using a singleton `do` structure, but I find this approach to be conceptually more explicit and easier to read. An important complication in all cases is that we do not want to `kill` or `spawn` snakes within the body of such an iterative loop; this would alter the very collection that we are currently iterating through and would immediately open the door to strange bugs and errors.

Finalizing the Controller

Now all that is left to do is initiate our Controller and provide a public interface. The responsibilities of the `init` method are to assign the Model and View (that should be passed as arguments) to the `model` and `view` variables respectively, to launch an agent for updating `gestalt` at regular intervals, to set up the View's `drawFunc` and `onCloseFunc` functions and to launch the agent responsible for updating the `population`. The code is trivial and can be found online in this book's code bundle.

And now we are ready to launch the last, and definitely the most complicated example of this book! Time to enjoy an ever changing organic population of snakes moving in all directions and producing all sorts of funny noises while leading their tiny artificial snake lives. Sometimes they are making love to each other to spawn new children (a fundamental and quite joyful activity of living creatures, by the way), killing each other (an equally fundamental, albeit not-so-joyful property of life) or simply ignoring each other (which sometimes seems like the most fundamental of all of life's properties).

A still from the animation is shown as follows

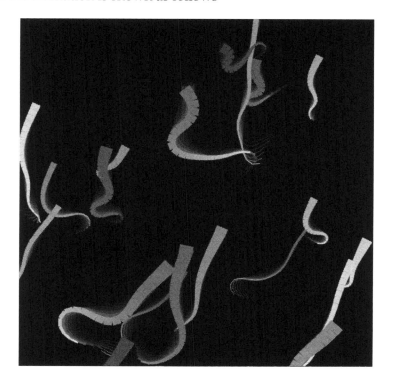

The following figure abstractly describes the entire architecture of our program:

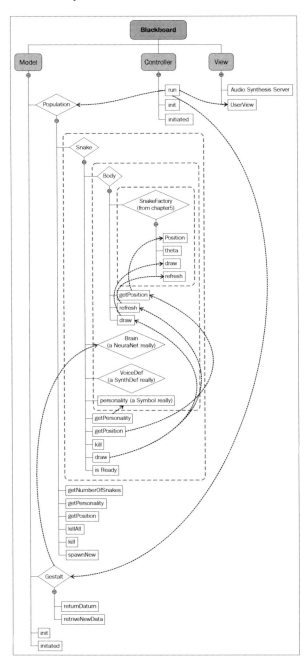

Summary

In this chapter we demonstrated how to deal with complicated real-life situations and apply certain methodologies to design and implement them. On occasions of a quite involved example, we illustrated how to break more complicated tasks into small parts and apply well-known programming patterns to easily and efficiently code and finalize it. It must be noted that some of these patterns have been used abusively hereinbefore, and in a rather broader sense, however, this chapter does not pretend to be an exhaustive treatise of such a subject but rather a hands-on introduction to an object-oriented way of thinking. Being pragmatic, we simply pinpointed how to solve real-life problems in efficient and elegant ways by means of well-known computer science paradigms.

Index

W

wave 24

Waveform

  aperiodic 26

  generators 29

  periodic 26

  scoping 14, 15

  synthesis fundamentals 24

  trailing 132

  transformations 33

Waveshaping

  about 34-36

  binary operations 38

  bitwise operations 39

  unary operations 36, 37

Wavetable lookup synthesis 29, 30

wavetables

  envelopes, using as 31, 32

weblog. *See* **blog**

windmills

  rotating 137, 138

wrappers 189

Z

ZeroCrossing 118

Thank you for buying
Mapping and Visualization with SuperCollider

About Packt Publishing

Packt, pronounced 'packed', published its first book "*Mastering phpMyAdmin for Effective MySQL Management*" in April 2004 and subsequently continued to specialize in publishing highly focused books on specific technologies and solutions.

Our books and publications share the experiences of your fellow IT professionals in adapting and customizing today's systems, applications, and frameworks. Our solution based books give you the knowledge and power to customize the software and technologies you're using to get the job done. Packt books are more specific and less general than the IT books you have seen in the past. Our unique business model allows us to bring you more focused information, giving you more of what you need to know, and less of what you don't.

Packt is a modern, yet unique publishing company, which focuses on producing quality, cutting-edge books for communities of developers, administrators, and newbies alike. For more information, please visit our website: www.packtpub.com.

About Packt Open Source

In 2010, Packt launched two new brands, Packt Open Source and Packt Enterprise, in order to continue its focus on specialization. This book is part of the Packt Open Source brand, home to books published on software built around Open Source licences, and offering information to anybody from advanced developers to budding web designers. The Open Source brand also runs Packt's Open Source Royalty Scheme, by which Packt gives a royalty to each Open Source project about whose software a book is sold.

Writing for Packt

We welcome all inquiries from people who are interested in authoring. Book proposals should be sent to author@packtpub.com. If your book idea is still at an early stage and you would like to discuss it first before writing a formal book proposal, contact us; one of our commissioning editors will get in touch with you.

We're not just looking for published authors; if you have strong technical skills but no writing experience, our experienced editors can help you develop a writing career, or simply get some additional reward for your expertise.

FusionCharts Beginner's Guide: The Official Guide for FusionCharts Suite

ISBN: 978-1-849691-76-5   Paperback: 252 pages

Create interactive charts in JavaScript (HTML5) and Flash for your web and enterprise applications

1. Go from nothing to delightful reports and dashboards in your web applications in super quick time

2. Create your first chart in 15 minutes and customize it both aesthetically and functionally

3. Create a powerful reporting experience with advanced capabilities like drill-down and JavaScript integration

Clojure Data Analysis Cookbook

ISBN: 978-1-782162-64-3   Paperback: 342 pages

Over 110 recipes to help you dive into the world of practical data analysis using Clojure

1. Get a handle on the torrent of data the modern Internet has created

2. Recipes for every stage from collection to analysis

3. A practical approach to analyzing data to help you make informed decisions

Please check **www.PacktPub.com** for information on our titles

OpenSceneGraph 3.0: Beginner's Guide

ISBN: 978-1-849512-82-4   Paperback: 412 pages

Create high-performance virtual reality applications with OpenSceneGraph, one of the best 3D graphics engine

1. Create high quality 2D plots by using Matplotlib productively

2. Incremental introduction to Matplotlib, from the ground up to advanced levels

3. Embed Matplotlib in GTK+, Qt, and wxWidgets applications as well as web sites to utilize them in Python applications

4. Deploy Matplotlib in web applications and expose it on the Web using popular web frameworks such as Pylons and Django

Statistical Analysis with R

ISBN: 978-1-849512-08-4   Paperback: 300 pages

Take control of your data and produce superior statistical analyses with R

1. An easy introduction for people who are new to R, with plenty of strong examples for you to work through

2. This book will take you on a journey to learn R as the strategist for an ancient Chinese kingdom!

3. A step by step guide to understand R, its benefits, and how to use it to maximize the impact of your data analysis

Please check **www.PacktPub.com** for information on our titles